INTERMEDIATE I
Hospitality
course notes

Alastair MacGregor

Text © 2007 Alastair MacGregor
Design and layout © 2007 Leckie & Leckie
Cover photo © G. Gauter/photocuisine/Corbis
Cover design by Caleb Rutherford

0101082007

ISBN 978-1-84372-475-9

Published by
Leckie & Leckie Ltd
3rd Floor, 4 Queen Street, Edinburgh EH2 1JE
Phone: 0131 220 6831   Fax: 0131 225 9987
enquiries@leckieandleckie.co.uk   www.leckieandleckie.co.uk

Special thanks to
Project One Publishing Solutions, Edinburgh (project management and editing)
The Partnership Publishing Solutions, Glasgow (design and page layout)
Ellustration (illustrations)

Printed in the UK by Nuffield Press

A CIP Catalogue record for this book is available from the British Library.

CONTENTS

Introduction

Welcome to *Intermediate 1 Hospitality (Practical Cookery) Course Notes.* This book will help you as your progress your way through your Intermediate 1 Hospitality: Practical Cookery course.

This book provides you with full coverage of all the content that is required for the course and is designed to help you to:

- develop an understanding of hygienic food handling
- plan your work to integrate practical skills
- develop your skills in food preparation techniques and cookery processes
- identify equipment used in food preparation and cooking
- know and understand the terms used in food preparation techniques and cookery processes
- understand the implications of food safety regulations for those involved in the hospitality and food industry.

The chapters of the book are arranged to cover the main areas of course content. The importance of safety and hygiene is regularly highlighted throughout the book. Practical cooking tips and useful facts and figures are included throughout.

Chapter 1: Kitchen Organisation

This chapter provides an insight into the professional kitchen. It combines both information and activities that will take you through the process of planning your work, requisitioning resources and costing recipes. These are skills and knowledge that you will be assessed on.

Chapter 2: Food Preparation

This chapter describes the basic food preparation techniques and equipment that you will be required to know about and demonstrate appropriate use of. You will be assessed on your knowledge of these aspects of food preparation, as well as specific cooking terms.

Chapter 3: Cookery Processes

This chapter describes the wet and dry cookery processes that you will be required to know and demonstrate in your course. These processes are described in terms of method, cooking medium, equipment and foods appropriate to each process.

Chapter 4: Food Safety

This chapter describes various aspects of food safety and hygiene – conditions for bacterial contamination, methods of food storage and preservation, and rules and regulations regarding food handling and premises in which food is prepared.

Course assessment

Intermediate 1 Hospitality: Practical Cookery does not have a final written examination, but you will be assessed in the component units that make up the course awards:

- Food hygiene for the hospitality industry
- Hospitality: Organisation of practical skills
- Food preparation techniques: An introduction
- Cookery processes: An introduction

Your course assessment is based on a practical assignment undertaken under controlled conditions. The assignment is set by the Scottish Qualifications Authority and will:

- incorporate a range of techniques, equipment, processes and ingredients
- involve the preparation of four portions of different dishes within a $1\frac{1}{2}$ hour period. The dishes will either be a starter and a main course or a main course and a dessert.

The practical assignment is worth 70 marks and will be assessed by your class teacher.

How to use this book

This book has a clear, easy-to-read layout with a number of features designed to help you understand the course.

For you to do   This feature provides you with a range of tasks and activities designed to test your knowledge of the content of the book. This feature also helps as a revision and consolidation activity.

Leckie & Leckie Learning Lab   This feature indicates when activities and web links mentioned in *For you to do* activities are listed on the Leckie & Leckie Learning Lab page. To find these, go to: www.leckieandleckie.co.uk, click on the Learning Lab button and navigate to the Intermediate 1 Hospitality Course Notes page.

Word bank   This feature explains or defines some of the important terms used in the book.

Hints and Tips   This feature provides you with some important points that will help you with your studies. These hints and tips will be about your course content or about steps that you can take to improve your practical skills.

Answers   Answers to the *For you to do* activities are given on pages 92–93.

Glossary   A glossary is given on pages 94–95, making it easy for you to quickly look up definitions and explanations .

CHAPTER 1
KITCHEN ORGANISATION

The Professional Kitchen

A well-run kitchen will prepare and cook the right amount of high quality food for the required number of people, on time, with the best use of staff, ingredients and equipment.

In the late 19th century, Auguste Escoffier devised the **partie system** for organising a professional kitchen, in which different sections of the kitchen were tasked to carry out specific jobs, whether preparing or cooking the fish, meat or vegetables.

Some kitchens today – particularly in large hotels – still use Escoffier's partie system, while others have adopted their own systems to suit smaller kitchen teams and less complex menus.

The flow chart below provides an example of how a kitchen might be organised using the partie system.

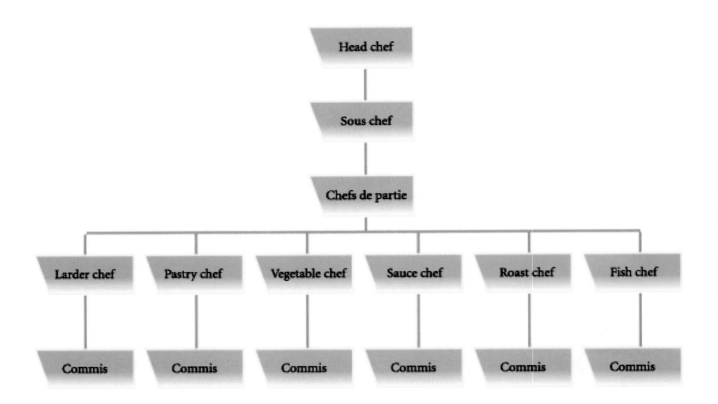

The **Head chef** is in charge of the kitchen. It is their responsibility to allocate the work between the different sections in the kitchen and to ensure that the results are of the expected standard.

The **Sous chef** is the assistant to the Head chef. A Sous chef will have a good knowledge of all the sections of the kitchen.

The **Chef de partie** is in charge of a section of work in the kitchen. This is the job of a specialist, for example, the person in charge of sauces or pastry/dessert.

The **Commis chef** is an assistant cook. The commis chef acts as an assistant to the Chef de partie.

Thinking About Food Safety and Hygiene

Personal hygiene should be simple and straightforward. The rules to be followed are common sense, but few people actually follow them.

Do You Know?

On average:

- 90% of people do not wash their hands before eating
- 25% wash their hands only with water and not soap
- 34% do not dry their hands after washing them
- 25% carry dangerous bacteria after leaving toilets but only 4% have them on entering.

Personal cleanliness is:
- your moral duty
- your legal duty
- something to be proud of.

Personal hygiene plays an important part in the day-to-day running of any food organisation.

Many types of **bacteria** that cause food poisoning live on or in our bodies, and it is important to follow some simple rules to try to prevent transferring them on to food.

Personal hygiene rules

- Bathe or shower daily.
- Wash hair regularly – including beards.
- Keep fingernails short, clean and do not wear nail varnish.
- Do not wear any jewellery as it may unfasten and fall into food or drink or could trap dirt.
- Do not wear strong perfume or aftershave as the smell may taint food.
- Have a clean change of clothing every day.
- Make sure that protective clothing provided for you is kept clean.
- Do not touch your nose, eyes, lips or hair, lick your fingers or bite your nails.
- Wash your hands after:

  - going to the toilet
  - a break in the rest-room
  - touching your face or hair
  - sneezing, coughing, or blowing your nose
  - cleaning duties
  - touching dirty surfaces or utensils
  - handling raw food
  - handling rubbish.

- Do not eat, drink, smoke or comb your hair in any food preparation area.
- Wear all protective clothing provided and change it daily.
- Cover minor cuts and **abrasions** with a suitable, brightly coloured waterproof dressing.
- A food worker who is suffering from, for example, diarrhoea, sickness, skin allergies or problems, should not be allowed to work with food. Such illnesses should be reported to a supervisor.

Effective Hand Washing

To ensure that your hands are spotlessly clean, follow these instructions.

Use a wash hand basin provided only for washing hands. It must have:

- hot water
- soap
- paper towels or other means of drying hands.

Make sure you wash:

- palms
- back of hands
- between fingers
- under nails.

In the interests of hygiene wash only <u>**hands**</u> here

Visitors to Kitchens

All visitors must comply with personal hygiene rules and this includes delivery staff.

> **Bacteria:** *very small organisms that live in the air, earth, water, or on the surface of things, some of which can cause disease.*
>
> **Moral duty:** *good and appropriate behaviour linked to a specific situation.*
>
> **Abrasion:** *where the surface of the skin has been rubbed away.*

For you to do

1 a Complete the word search on hygiene terms on the Leckie and Leckie website. Go to: www.leckieandleckie.co.uk, click on the Learning Lab button and navigate to the Intermediate 1 Hospitality Course Notes page.

LECKIE&LECKIE *Learning Lab*

b Design a poster to be displayed in a kitchen to encourage people to wash their hands correctly.

Planning Your Work

Effective planning and organisation of your work is the key to success.

Planning can greatly reduce your stress levels. Proper planning gives you the peace of mind of knowing that you have developed a feasible or workable plan of action that allows you to complete tasks given to you.

Because part of the planning process involves creating a **contingency** plan, planning allows you to be prepared for things that go wrong or for unexpected problems.

> **Effective:** *useful; produces a good result.*
> **Contingency:** *back-up, in case things don't work out as planned or intended.*

Planning also helps you evaluate your progress as you work. Planning activities will let you see whether or not you are staying on schedule.

When planning your work there are a number of key terms that you need to be familiar with:

- **task:** a piece of work to be undertaken or completed, for example, a recipe
- **components:** the ingredients
- **processes:** the steps that have to be undertaken to complete the dish.

Let's look at each of these in more detail, using a specific example – the task of making a coffee and chocolate mousse for four people.

Hints and Tips

Generally, you should be selecting recipes that have more than five components. You should also select recipes that have more than six processes. Remember that there can be more than one process in each stage of the method.

The Task

Your task is to make a coffee and chocolate mousse that should serve four people.

First, look at the recipe for coffee and chocolate mousse to identify the component parts and the processes.

Recipe: Coffee and chocolate mousse

Ingredients

Corn flour	50g
Cocoa powder	30g
Skimmed milk	600ml
Honey	30ml
Coffee powder	10g
Glacé cherries	8

The ingredients are the component parts. This task has six component parts.

Each of the main steps in the method are the processes, for example:
- blending the corn flour and cocoa powder
- simmering the mixture for 3–4 minutes.

Serves: 8
Cooking time: 3–4 minutes

Method

1 Blend the corn flour and the cocoa powder with 120ml of milk in a large bowl.
2 Heat the remainder of the milk in a pan with the honey and coffee powder, stirring until the honey has dissolved.
3 Just before the milk boils, pour over the corn flour mixture, stirring all the time.
4 Return the mixture to the pan and bring to the boil.
5 Simmer for 3–4 minutes and remove from the heat.
6 Place the pan in a basin of cold water and stir for 2–3 minutes to cool.
7 Spoon into bowl or serving dishes and top with glacé cherries.
8 Place in the fridge to set.

For you to do

2 Study the recipe below.
   a What is the task?
   b What are the component parts?
   c How many processes does this recipe have?

Fruit cooler

Ingredients	Method
1 orange	1 Collect all the ingredients.
1 x 5ml lemon juice	2 Wash the orange and cut into pieces.
250ml cold water	3 Place all the ingredients into a liquidiser
1 x 5ml caster sugar	4 Liquidise on a high speed for 20 seconds.
2 ice cubes	5 Drain through a sieve.
	6 Serve in chilled glasses.
Serves: 1	

Developing a Plan of Work

Now you know the meaning of the terms involved in planning your work, you can look at how to develop a plan of work, using the coffee and chocolate mousse as an example.

Imagine you have been given 50 minutes to collect all the ingredients and equipment for this recipe, then prepare and serve the mousse. You would need to complete a time plan sheet similar to the one below. The purpose of the time plan sheet is to allow you to plan and time the sequence of processes that you will have to complete when carrying out this task.

Times are normally allocated in blocks of 5 minutes. You should try to divide your task into easily identified stages. These stages will combine a number of processes.

This column is useful for making notes such as oven temperatures and the finishing times of cooking processes.

Times	Activities	Notes
10.00 – 10.05	Wash hands; collect ingredients.	
10.05 – 10.10	Prepare ingredients for blending.	
10.10 – 10.20	Make the sauce and simmer. Cool mixture.	
10.20 – 10.25	Tidy work surface.	
10.25 – 10.30	Pour mousse into serving dishes and decorate. Chill in fridge.	Chill until 10.45
10.30 – 10.45	Clear table, wash, dry and put away dishes.	
10.45 – 10.50	Serve coffee and chocolate mousse.	

It is important to plan time to tidy the work area and for washing dishes during the task.

Hints and Tips

Careful and effective planning is always important to the success of a task. It is a good idea to read over all recipes carefully so that you fully understand each part of the recipe. It is also a good idea when you have completed a time plan to run through it before any assessment. That way you can pre-test your time plan to make sure it works!

For you to do

3 Using the recipe provided for the Fruit cooler, produce a time plan for the preparation and serving of this dish. Your time plan should start at 2 pm and finish at 2.20 pm.

Do You Know

There is a famous story about King Alfred the Great who was asked to look after some cakes that were cooking in the oven. He was in the middle of planning a battle and so forgot about the cakes and they burned. Perhaps if he had made a time plan first he might not have forgotten about the cakes!

Requisitioning

Once you have identified the task, the components and the processes, the next stage is to **requisition** all the resources you need in order to complete the task.

Requisitioning simply means ordering. For a task you will need to requisition:

- food ingredients
- special equipment, for example, food processor, microwave cooker
- any other resources, for example, lining paper, cake cases.

It is important to remember that you need to requisition only the amounts of food, equipment and resources that you need to complete the task. Some recipes may list more quantities of ingredients than you need (for example, the recipe for coffee and chocolate mousse serves eight, whereas your task is to serve four). If this happens, you need to adjust your requisition accordingly.

Let's look at the recipe for coffee and chocolate mousse again and work through the process of requisitioning food, equipment and resources.

Recipe: Coffee and chocolate mousse

Ingredients

Corn flour	50g
Cocoa powder	30g
Skimmed milk	600ml
Honey	30ml
Coffee powder	10g
Glacé cherries	8

These are the food items that need to be requisitioned (ordered).
This recipe is for 8 portions, so the ingredients need to be halved to make 4 portions.

There are no specific items of equipment or special resources that need to be ordered for the recipe on page 11. But if you wished to decorate the mousse with whipped cream you would need to order a piping bag and star tube (as well as cream).

When requisitioning food, equipment and resources you will generally be asked to complete a **food requisition sheet**. An example has been completed opposite for the coffee and chocolate mousse recipe.

FOOD REQUISITION SHEET

Name: .... Chris Ryan .... Class: ... S3 P1 ......

Teacher: .... Mr Cook .... Date required: 11 November ....

Item(s) to be made: .... Coffee and chocolate mousse ....

Meat and Fish	Quantity	Fruit and Vegetables	Quantity
Dairy Products Skimmed milk	Quantity 300ml	**Tins/Bottles/Dried** Glacé cherries Cocoa powder Honey Coffee powder Corn flour	Quantity 4 15g 15ml 5g 25g
Other foods	Quantity	**Equipment and Resources**	

The quantites have been halved.

You only use this section to order specialist equipment. You do not need to order equipment that is provided in your work area.

For you to do

4 Using a blank requisition sheet (your own or one downloaded from the Learning Lab section of the Leckie and Leckie website), place the following foods, equipment and resources into the correct section.

LECKIE&LECKIE Learning Lab

30g butter	½ lettuce
8 chicken thighs	1 small melon
2 sprigs of rosemary	225g seedless grapes
150ml chicken stock	50ml olive oil
2 sticks celery	microwave oven
30ml tarragon vinegar	pepper mill grinder

Hints and Tips

When requisitioning foods, double-check your recipes to make sure that you have not forgotten anything. If you have not ordered a food item, the recipe will not work.

Costing

So far, the coffee and chocolate mousse recipe has been used to help you to understand what is meant by:

- tasks
- component parts
- processes
- requisitioning
- planning your work.

The same recipe is used to help you to understand what we mean by **food costing**.

In the hospitality industry it is important to know how much it costs to produce different dishes that appear on a menu. This ensures that items on the menu are priced appropriately. It also helps with budgeting procedures within the restaurant or kitchen.

First, there are a few important points to remember.

1   You need to check how many portions the recipe is for. This recipe is for 8 portions.

2   You will normally be cooking food which will serve 4 portions.

3   You need to work out the cost of producing 4 portions of a recipe, before working out the cost of 1 portion.

4   In order to get up-to-date prices for food items, try using the internet, for example, the websites of supermarkets. For links to websites, go to the Learning Lab page on the Leckie and Leckie website.

5   Round prices up when the cost is above 0.5 pence, for example, round 1.67p up to 2p.

6   Round prices down when the cost is below 0.5 pence, for example, round 1.2p down to 1p.

7   There is a basic costing formula to use:

$$\frac{\text{unit cost}}{\text{unit price}} \times \text{quantity required}$$

The following example shows how to work out the cost of making one portion of the coffee and chocolate mousse recipe.

Recipe: Coffee and chocolate mousse

Ingredients

Corn flour	50g
Cocoa powder	30g
Skimmed milk	600ml
Honey	30ml
Coffee powder	10g
Glacé cherries	8

Serves: 8

This recipe serves 8 portions. You need to serve 4 portions so divide all ingredient weights by 2.

RECIPE COSTING SHEET

Dish: ....

Portions required: *The number of portions specified in the task.*

Recipe portions: *The number of portions specified in the recipe.*

Ingredients	Recipe measures		Actual measures		Costing	
	Units	Millilitres/ Grams	Units	Millilitres/ Grams	Unit/Litre/ kg price	Total cost
					Cost	
					Cost per portion	

The ingredients used in the recipe.

The measurements used in the recipe. This can be in grams, millilitres or units, e.g. $^1/_2$ can.

The actual measurements you need to serve 4 portions.

The cost of the food item, e.g. 39p for a 300g can.

The actual cost of the ingredient for the quantity used in the recipe.

The total cost of the recipe to make for 4 portions.

The cost per portion. Divide the total cost by 4.

Now let's fill in all the columns and do all the calculations.

RECIPE COSTING SHEET

Dish: Coffee and chocolate mousse

Portions required: 4   Recipe portions: 8

Ingredients	Recipe measures		Actual measures		Costing	
	Units	Millilitres/ Grams	Units	Millilitres/ Grams	Unit/Litre/ kg price	Total cost
Corn flour		50g		25g	500g/69p	£0.03
Cocoa powder		30g		15g	240g/125p	£0.08
Skimmed milk		600ml		300ml	3400ml/162p	£0.06
Honey		30ml		15ml	340g/115p	£0.05
Coffee powder		10g		5g	200g/365p	£0.09
Glacé cherries	8		4		200g/112p	£0.11
					Cost	£0.42
					Cost per portion	£0.11

Total cost of 4 portions = £0.42
Total cost of 1 portion = £0.42 / 4 = 10.5p
Total cost of 1 portion = £0.11 (rounded up)

Example calculation: cocoa powder

Cocoa powder costs £1.25, or 125 pence for 240 grams.

To get the cost of 1 gram we divide the cost of the cocoa powder by the weight of the cocoa powder: 125p ÷ 240 grams

This gives a total of 0.52 pence for 1 gram of cocoa powder.

The recipe uses 15 grams of cocoa powder and so we multiply the cost of one gram (0.52p) by 15: 0.52 × 15

This gives a total of 7.8 pence for the amount needed by the recipe.

This needs to be rounded up to the nearest penny and so the total cost of the cocoa powder is 8 pence (or £0.08).

You should follow this same process to cost all the ingredients in the recipe.

Go to the Learning Lab page on the Leckie and Leckie website if you want to see the full set of calculations.

For you to do

5 Look at the ingredients listed below to make a sponge cake. The recipe is for 4 portions. Work out how much it will cost to make 2 portions using the prices provided.

Ingredients for a sponge cake

100g margarine
100g self-raising flour
100g caster sugar
2 eggs

Cost of ingredients

Self-raising flour	50 pence for 1500g
Caster sugar	75 pence for 1000g
Margarine	50 pence for 500g
Eggs	£1.00 for 10 eggs

Hints and Tips

When costing food, rather than having to go to the supermarket, use the internet and log on to one of the major supermarket on line shopping sites. You can look up product prices there – and even find the best buys. For links to some supermarket websites, go to the Leckie and Leckie Learning Lab page.

Weighing and Measuring

Accurate measuring of ingredients is important to successful cooking and baking. Some foods can be affected by too much or too little of certain ingredients, such as salt, baking soda, baking powder and hot or spicy ingredients, such as chilli powder. When weighing and measuring ingredients you will need to measure either dry or liquid ingredients. You also need to measure small or large quantities of either dry or liquid ingredients. The following information will help you measure your ingredients accurately.

You will usually find that the weights and measures used in a recipe are given in **metric measurements**, that is, the weights and measurements will be given as:

- grams (g)
- kilograms (kg)
- millilitres (ml)
- litres (l).

However, some older recipe books will provide weights and measures using different systems of measurements, for example:

- cups (American and Australian measures)
- ounces and pounds (imperial weights used many years ago in the UK).

It is important that you always use metric weights and measures. Use the conversion charts on page 96 of this book to convert non-metric measures to metric measures.

Measuring Spoons

Measuring spoons come in all shapes and sizes, but they usually consist of a set of four spoons which can be made from different materials such as plastic or metal.

Measuring spoons are used to measure small quantities of dry and liquid ingredients. It is useful to have two sets so that one can be used for dry ingredients and one can be used for liquid ingredients. This prevents having to wash and dry the spoons after using them for liquid ingredients before using with the next dry ingredient.

Measuring spoons tend to include basic measures of:

- 1.25ml ($\frac{1}{4}$ teaspoon)
- 2.5ml ($\frac{1}{2}$ teaspoon)
- 5ml (1 teaspoon)
- 15ml (1 tablespoon).

However, different sets may come with different measuring sizes.

Hints and Tips

When using measuring spoons to measure an ingredient, hold the spoon flat and pour the ingredient into the spoon until it reaches the top rim of the spoon.

Measuring Cups

Measuring cups tend to be either plastic or metal cups of various sizes used for single measures. There are also adjustable measuring cups available. Measuring cups are used to measure dry ingredients, such as flour, sugar, oats, rice and solid ingredients, such as margarine and jam. Measuring cups are also used to measure liquids.

The single measure cups generally measure:

- $\frac{1}{4}$ cup (60ml)
- $\frac{1}{3}$ cup (80ml)
- $\frac{1}{2}$ cup (125ml)
- 1 cup (250ml).

Measuring Jugs

Measuring jugs tend to be glass or clear plastic containers with a spout for pouring and a handle. They are available in a range of sizes, with the smallest commonly being 250ml. Jugs usually have graduated scales on the side to help measure quantities. The spout on the jug assists in pouring the contents when adding to other ingredients.

Hints and Tips

When measuring liquids, have the measuring jug sitting on a flat, level surface and bend down to view the measurement at eye level. Do not hold the jug up to eye level because you might not hold the jug level when viewing, which may result in an inaccurate reading.

You can also buy glass and plastic measuring jugs that are large enough to be used as mixing bowls. They are similar to measuring jugs in that they have a spout, handle, and measurement scale down the side. They work well for large tasks and can be used for mixing and pouring batters, such as pancake or waffle batter.

Scales

Scales are a kitchen device used to measure the weight of ingredients and other foods. A scale measures ingredients more accurately than if you measure them by volume (such as cups). Scales are available in manual and digital models

Balance or spring scales are used to measure the weight of ingredients. Digital scales will be more accurate than manual scales and can measure both smaller and larger amounts of ingredients.

Digital scales   *Manual scales*

Manual scales can be less accurate than digital scales but are useful when you need to weigh large amounts of ingredients. You can buy manual scales in different sizes. When you need to measure small amounts of foods, make sure that you are using manual scales that measure in amounts of at least 2 grams.

Measuring Terminology

Recipes will sometimes use specific terms to indicate how much of an ingredient should be added to a recipe. These terms include:

- **pinch:** a measurement used with dry ingredients such as herbs, which is the amount you can pinch between your forefinger and thumb
- **dash:** a small amount of an ingredient when measuring dry ingredients; a dash used to measure liquid ingredients equals approximately three drops
- **heaped:** a term indicating that as much dry ingredient should be added in the measure as you can so that it heaps over the rim of the measuring cup or spoon.

For you to do

1 Suggest what weighing or measuring equipment you would use to measure the following ingredients:

   a 225 g flour

   b 125 ml milk

   c 1000 g sugar

   d 1.25 ml curry powder

   e 300 g tinned chopped tomatoes

   f 15 ml soy sauce

Handy Measures

It is important to measure and weigh food ingredients accurately, particularly when you are looking for a good end result when following a recipe. However, there are also times when you might want to use what we call **handy measures**. They are a quick way to measure ingredients without having to use scales or measuring spoons, and are useful when measurements don't have to be accurate.

Handy measures include:

■ **tablespoon:** when referring to dry goods, such as flour, this usually means a rounded tablespoon (see below)

■ **level tablespoon:** this is where the ingredient being measured is just level with the top edge of the spoon – fill the spoon and then run a knife across the top two edges of the spoon, scraping off any excess

■ **rounded tablespoon:** this means there is as much of the ingredient in the bowl of the spoon as there is above the top edge of the spoon

■ **heaped tablespoon:** this means as much ingredient as possible on the spoon without it falling off.

Handy Spoon Measures

■ 1 tablespoon = 3 teaspoons

■ 1 dessertspoon = 2 teaspoons

■ 1 level tablespoon = 15ml

■ 1 level teaspoon = 5ml

Use this table when measuring about **25g** of the ingredients listed.

Ingredient	Number of level tablespoons
Breadcrumbs (fresh)	6
Cheese (grated)	5
Cocoa powder	4
Flour	3
Honey	1
Icing sugar (sifted)	3
Porridge oats	4
Rice	2
Salt	1
Sugar (granulated)	2

Hints and Tips

If measurements need to be accurate, remember to use proper weighing and measuring equipment, not handy measures.

Be careful when reading recipes, and don't confuse the abbreviations of a tablespoon (tbsp) and teaspoon (tsp).

Measuring Butter and Margarine

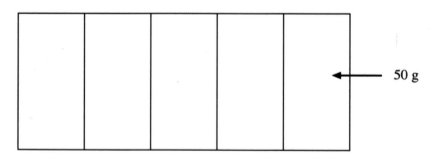

← 50 g

There is a quick handy method to measure margarine or butter.

Margarine, butter and lard tend to be sold in 250g blocks. Open the pack of butter, margarine or lard and gently mark out this layout or grid on top, dividing it into five equal amounts (50g).

For you to do

2 Draw a diagram similar to the one above to show how would you mark a block of butter to get:

a 25g   **b** 12.5g

Food Preparation Equipment

The use of food preparation equipment is an important stage between fresh food coming into the kitchen and being made ready for either cooking or direct service to customers in a café or restaurant. The equipment ranges from the simple potato peeler to the more complex and expensive multi-function food processors.

This section looks at the basic food preparation equipment that you will use in your practical cookery course. Many of the items of equipment are illustrated (but remember that different manufacturers may have slight variations on the ones shown here). There is a description of how each item of equipment is used in food preparation, along with additional information enabling you to develop a deeper understanding of food preparation equipment.

The equipment is listed in alphabetical order to make it easy for you to find.

Cooling Tray

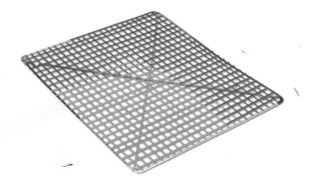

Main use

A cooling tray is used to allow hot cooked food to cool on all sides. Food can be placed directly on to the cooling tray or it can still be in a cooking pan.

Additional information

A cooling tray is usually made of stainless steel wires that are shaped into a network of squares or a number of straight, parallel lines so that food being cooled can easily be held without falling through. At the same time, air circulates underneath the food, cooling the food so it does not become soggy.

Electric Food Processor

Main use

An electric food processor is a multi-functional utensil. It can blend, chop, grate, mince, purée and slice a range of food ingredients. Some can even knead dough.

Additional information

Food processors have a range of detachable blades which are used for the different processes. Having different blades and attachments matched to different processes means that the processor is able to do lots of tasks very well, and can also be cleaned easily. Because the food processor is so quick, it is a very handy tool in the kitchen.

Fish Slice

Main use

A fish slice is used to turn food over during cooking, for example while shallow frying, and to remove cooked food items from pots and pans. Fish slices are available in a number of shapes and sizes, depending on what they are used for. Usually made of  stainless steel, the blade might be narrow, long, wide, or slotted, and it might be stiff or flexible, again depending on the task (stiff blades for heavier foods and flexible blades for lighter and more delicate foods such as eggs and fish). The handle may be long and straight or angled so the blade can be placed easily into a pan with hot oils or ingredients while keeping fingers or hands away from the hot pan and food.

Additional information

The blades of some fish slices are slotted or have holes in them so that excess liquid can drain away. If handling delicate items such as fried eggs, potatoes or fish, you might need a fish slice with a wider or longer blade so you can hold the food safely and easily held while excess liquid drains away. Slotted fish slices can be used when grilling – these are made with longer handles so your hands don't get too close to the hot grill.

Flour Dredger

Main use

A dredger is a metal container with a cover/lid that has small holes punched in it. It is used for sprinkling a light coating of flour on a work board, for example, when making pastry.

Additional information

You can also get a sugar dredger which can be used to sprinkle a light coat of caster sugar or icing sugar. This looks very similar to a flour dredger but the size of the holes punched in the lid will vary depending on the type of sugar to be used.

Grater

Main use

A grater is a kitchen tool for food preparation that grates and shreds food finely so the ingredient can be evenly mixed into the food being prepared.

Additional information

There are many different types of grater available, all of which have specific uses. An all-purpose grater or box grater generally has several sides, with each side having a different grating pattern suitable for different foods and purposes. Some graters have a side or section that can be used for slicing.

Rasp grater

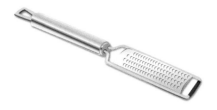

The flat hand or rasp grater is hand held so it can be easily moved across the food being grated, with the food gratings collecting underneath. Hand graters can be flat or curved to suit the item to be grated. They can also be used to grate or **zest** small amounts of citrus peels.

Zesting: *where a very fine amount of skin is removed from a citrus fruit such as a lemon, by gently rubbing the skin over the fine grating surface.*

Hints and Tips

Store lemon, orange and lime rinds in the freezer. Simple grate the frozen rind whenever you need it.

Rotary grater

A rotary grater is a hand-held tool that consists of a handle or turning mechanism, a food compartment and a cylindrical grating surface. A small amount of food is placed into a holding unit next to the grating surface. The handle is turned manually, causing the cylindrical drum to rotate over the surface of the food, grating it as it moves. The rotary grater is also known as a **mouli grater** or **cheese grater** and is especially useful for grating hard or dense cheese, such as Parmesan.

Knife

Knives should always be kept sharp. Sharp knives are safer than blunt knives. The normal **construction** of a good quality knife is shown below. Different knives have different sizes, shapes and cutting edges, depending on their uses.

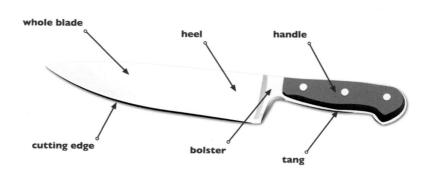

Construction: *the process of building something.*

whole blade

heel

handle

cutting edge

bolster

tang

Cook's knife

Main use

A cook's knife is a general-purpose knife that is used for most types of chopping, dicing and slicing.

Additional information

Sometimes known as a **chef's knife** or **French knife**, this knife has a blade that ranges in length from over 15cm to 30cm in length. The feel, weight and balance of this knife allow it to be used for heavy duty work with thicker cuts of vegetables, fruits, meats and fresh herbs.

Vegetable knife

Main use

A vegetable knife is a smaller knife that is used for trimming and shaping vegetables, and also for peeling and coring foods or cutting small items. It is also known as a **paring knife**.

Additional Information

This is a small knife with a straight, sharp blade that is usually 9–10cm long. Its thin, narrow blade is pointed at the tip. Its small size makes it easy to handle and it is ideal when working with small bits of food or small ingredients, such as shallots and garlic.

Palette knife

Main use

A palette knife is a blunt-style knife that is used for shaping, lifting and turning foods as well as spreading, smoothing and finishing surfaces, for example, when icing cakes.

Additional information

A palette knife has a rounded, non-cutting edge and comes in a variety of different sizes between 10cm and 30cm.

Pastry Brush

Main use

A pastry brush is a 2.5cm or wider brush made with nylon or natural bristles. The brush is used to glaze the surface of items before or after cooking in order to give a flavoured coating, often with a sheen. It can be used to glaze biscuits and breads, as well as coating savoury items with oils, egg washes and sauces.

Additional information

Brush bristles vary in type and quality. Brushes made of boars hair are best, because they are more absorbent than nylon bristles, and keep their shape better. Most brushes have plastic or rubber handles, allowing the brush to be easily hand- or machine-washed. Some brushes have wooden handles but these need more care as they usually need to be washed by hand.

Pastry Cutter

Main use

A pastry cutter is a hand-held tool used to cut evenly shaped pieces from pastry, biscuit or cookie dough when they are being prepared for baking.

Additional information

A cutter is usually made from stainless steel or plastic materials that easily cut through the dough. Pastry cutters are available in various dimensions that range in sizes of 5 cm upwards in diameter. Cutters are often designed to fit or nest inside each other to make them easy and tidy to store. You can also buy novelty cutters in different shapes, such as hearts, animals, etc.

Pastry wheel

A pastry wheel is used to cut pastry dough into required shapes prior to baking. The pastry wheel may have one or two wheels, made of wood or metal, which are attached to a handle. One wheel has a sharp, plain edge for marking and cutting the dough in a straight line. The optional second wheel has a sharp, patterned edge used for giving items such as ravioli and folded pastries a decorative edge.

Piping Bag

Main use

A piping bag is a cone-shaped bag that can be filled with cream, dough or creamed potato which is forced though a small opening to produce a decorative or fancy shape.

Additional information

Sometimes called a **pastry bag** or **icing bag**, a piping bag has a small opening on one end and a large opening on the opposite end. The large end is used for filling the bag with a mass of soft food, such as biscuit dough, frosting, whipped cream or creamed potato. The bag is squeezed, forcing the soft contents through the small opening. Decorative nozzles can be attached to the smaller opening, so, as the whipped cream, for example, is pushed through the opening, it can be shaped into a decorative finish. (See page 34 for more information about tubes and nozzles.) Piping bags and tubes/nozzles are used for making biscuits and pastries, for decorating cakes, and for filling pastries such as éclairs or doughnuts. The bag itself can be made of different types of material, such as polyester and nylon.

Rolling Pin

Main use

A rolling pin is a long, **cylindrical** utensil, generally used to roll out various types of dough when making bread, pastry and biscuits.

Additional information

A rolling pin also works well for crushing biscuits and nuts and making breadcrumbs. Wooden rolling pins are most common, but they can also be **ceramic** or made of marble, porcelain, glass, brass and copper.

> Cylindrical: *shaped like a cylinder.*
> Ceramic: *material produced by shaping and heating clay.*

Hints and Tips

Use a rolling pin for crushing biscuits and nuts. Put the biscuits into a plastic bag and place on to a chopping board. Gently break up the biscuits using the rolling pin. Remember to seal the bag before crushing, otherwise the contents will spill everywhere!

Sieve

Main use

A sieve is a kitchen tool used to strain liquid or to sift dry ingredients, such as flour or icing sugar.

Additional information

Sieves are made from different materials including stainless steel, aluminium, nylon, and cloth. Some sieves have heat-resistant handles and strong frames with hooks, which allow the sieve to sit on top of pots or bowls.

The **mesh** dome is the main part of the sieve and comes in different mesh sizes from medium to fine and superfine.

Sieves with a medium mesh are good for straining liquids away from, for example, pasta or vegetables.

Sieves with a fine mesh are good for straining less dense fluids and holding items such as fruit seeds.

Mesh: *net-like material with spaces in it.*

Sieves with a superfine mesh are good for straining very clear liquids and those containing fine particles. They can also be used to dust powder such as cocoa or icing sugar on baked goods.

Tablespoon

Main use

The tablespoon has a number of different uses in the kitchen. It can be used as a handy measure for measuring dry or liquid ingredients. It can also be used to mix food ingredients together, to stir foods together, and to fold ingredients together.

Additional information

When measuring liquids, it is generally accepted that a tablespoon is equivalent to 15ml of liquid. You can now buy plastic measuring spoons which provide additional measures usually ranging from 1.25ml ($\frac{1}{4}$ tsp) to 15ml (1 tablespoon).

Hints and Tips

Remember that a metal spoon conducts heat. If you use a metal spoon for stirring hot liquids the heat will travel through the spoon and this could cause a burn.

Tubes

A tube (or nozzle) is placed into the small end of a piping bag and held in position by the small hole that allows only the tip of the tube to exit the bag. The ingredients are pushed from the bag, going through the tube and, depending on the tube, formed into different shapes and lines, even writing, on the surface being decorated. (See page 31 for more information on piping bags.) The most common tubes are the plain tube and the star tube.

Plain tube

A plain tube can come in many different sizes. Small tubes are used for fine and decorative work. A plain tube with a much larger opening can be used for piping potatoes or doughs such as choux pastry for éclairs that would be too thick for fine piping.

Star tube

The star tube gives a textured or stamped or star shaped finish to the ingredients piped through.

A star tube can come in many different sizes. Small star tubes are used for fine and decorative work. Larger star tubes are used for piping potatoes, doughs, double cream or meringue that would be too thick for fine piping.

Vegetable Peeler

Main use

A vegetable peeler is a kitchen tool used to remove very thin layers of skin or flesh from vegetables such as potatoes and carrots and firm fruits, such as apples and pears.

Additional information

Different types of vegetable peelers are available. One type has a **rigid** blade that does not move, so the hand is required to move the peeler across the surface of the item being peeled.

Another type of peeler has a **swivel** blade, as shown in the picture above. The blade can adjust to the shape and surface of the item being peeled, allowing a thinner layer to be removed. Using this type of peeler is often quicker than using the rigid-blade peeler.

> **Rigid:** *stiff or fixed.*
> **Swivel:** *to turn round from a central point to face another direction.*

Hints and Tips

You probably know you can buy an egg slicer which will slice hard boiled eggs quickly and effectively. But did you know that it can also be used to slice some soft fruits such as kiwi fruits or soft vegetables such as mushrooms?

Whisks

Whisks are available in different shapes and sizes, and are used for different purposes. Some of the most common manual whisks are the rotary whisk, the flat whisk, the ball whisk and the balloon whisk.

Rotary whisk

A rotary whisk is a hand-held double whisk which is turned by hand and used to mix or beat ingredients together quickly or to incorporate air into ingredients such as egg whites or heavy cream in order to increase the volume of the mixture.

Flat whisk

A flat whisk is used for beating and mixing ingredients in pans or dishes with shallow sides. The flat whisk can be easily bent to the flat or rounded shape of a pan in order to stir or mix ingredients at the bottom or sides of the pan.

Ball whisk

A ball whisk is mostly used to blend sauces, whip eggs and stir batters. Each wire on the whisk has a weighted ball on the end, so the whisk can stir ingredients well, bending and shaping to the contour of the container in which the ingredients are mixed.

Balloon whisk

The balloon whisk is used for whipping light food ingredients, increasing the amount of air in the foods being whipped, such as egg whites, sauces or cream.

Hand-held electric whisk or mixer

Main use

A hand-held electric whisk has a pair of rotating beaters. A hand-mixer is used to beat, whip, and evenly combine ingredients such as those needed for sponge mixes and meringues.

Additional information

Hand-mixers usually have a range of speeds; sometimes these are indicated low, medium and high speeds, sometimes they are numbered. Having more speeds gives you more control over the mixing process. Some hand-held mixers have different attachments, such as dough hooks, spatulas and sifters.

For you to do

3 Complete the crossword on food preparation equipment on the Leckie and Leckie website. Go to: www.leckieandleckie.co.uk, click on the Learning Lab button and navigate to the Intermediate 1 Hospitality Course Notes page.

Food Preparation Techniques

A chef is only as good as the food he or she puts on the plate. The food presented on a plate is a sign of a chef's ability. The key to this is a good knowledge of food preparation techniques and an understanding of when and how they should be used. This section looks at the food preparation techniques that you will be assessed on, including the equipment needed to perform the technique. These food preparation techniques will be demonstrated by your teacher or lecturer and you will also have time to practise these.

Peel

The outer skin of a fruit or vegetable is called 'peel', so peeling is the removal of this skin (called 'rind' in some instances). Depending on the nature of the skin and what the fruit or vegetable is being used for, sometimes the skin is removed, but sometimes it is left in place. The peel of some fruit contains essential aromatic oils, which can be used to flavour both sweet and savoury dishes.

A **vegetable peeler** is most commonly used to peel fruit and vegetables. However there are other items of equipment that can be used for peeling, such as orange or citrus peelers and julienne peelers.

Orange or citrus peeler

This is a small, narrow tool used to remove the peel of citrus fruits such as oranges, lemons and limes.

Hints and Tips

To remove onion and garlic smells from your fingers after preparation, rub your fingers over the inside of a stainless steel sink. Sounds weird – but it does work!

Do You Know?

The outer skin of a citrus fruit is known as the **zest**. This contains essential oils which give foods flavour. Directly underneath the zest is the **pith** – a white layer of skin that can have a very bitter flavour. When zesting a citrus fruit you are removing only the very thin top layer of the skin.

Julienne peeler

A julienne peeler is used to make **julienne strips** – for decorative garnishes made of thin strips of fruits and vegetables. Julienne strips are usually very thin and are matchstick-sized, but can be cut to any length.

Hints and Tips

You can use a vegetable knife for peeling the skin from some vegetables, for example, potatoes, but you need to make sure that you are peeling only very thin strips of peel from the food. The main reasons for this are:

- most of the nutrients (vitamins) in fruits and vegetables are contained close to the skin
- peeling thick slices of skin from fruits and vegetables is wasteful.

Cut

Cutting is the process of breaking the surface of something, or to divide or make something smaller, using a sharp tool, especially a knife.

The knife is the most commonly used tool for cutting. Knives come in different shapes and sizes, for example, vegetable knife or cooks knife. See pages 29–30 for more information about knives.

Slice

To slice means to cut, generally across the food item, into thin pieces that are similar in thickness. Slices will most often range from 2mm to 4mm in thickness.

A **cooks knife** or a slicing knife is most commonly used to slice. These can come in different sizes. A **vegetable knife** can also be used for slicing small items. A **food processor** can also be used to slice food.

Hints and Tips

Place a damp paper towel under your chopping board to keep it from moving when preparing food.

Grate

Grating is the process of rubbing solid, firm food items such as cheese or carrots against a grating instrument to produce much smaller pieces or shreds. It is important to use the correct side of the grater so that you get the appropriate size of grated pieces. For example, when grating (zesting) the outer skin of a lemon you should use the finest side of the grater.

The item of kitchen equipment most commonly used to grate is a **grater**. A **food processor** is also able to grate food and may be better for food items that are difficult to grate on a manual grater or for large quantities.

Roll Out

Rolling out is the process of taking a pastry, biscuit or cookie dough and making it thinner and smoother, ready for shaping.

When rolling a dough, the rolling pin and surface should be lightly floured to prevent the dough from sticking. When rolling, begin to roll the dough starting from the centre and rolling away from you, stretching the dough gently as you roll. Move the pastry round clockwise after each roll, always starting at the centre and rolling away from you. You should continue rolling until the dough has the desired thickness.

A **rolling pin** is most commonly used to roll out pastry or dough.

Hints and Tips

You should never lift the pastry up and turn it over onto its other side. This will stretch the pastry and cause it to shrink when cooked.

Shape

Shaping is the process of taking food ingredients, for example, a beef burger mix, pastry dough or fishcake mix, and forming them into an appropriate shape depending on what you are making. Shaping can achieved in a number of different ways:

- shaping with hands or a palette knife to make fish cakes or beef burgers
- shaping a cake by using a knife to cut it into the required size and shape
- using pastry cutters to shape biscuits, scones and cookies.

Shaping pasta

Shaping biscuit mix

Shaping bread mix

Shaping shortbread

The most common items of kitchen equipment used for shaping are **cutters,** flan rings and cake tins. A **piping bag** can also be used for shaping, for example, piping a dough mix to make éclairs.

Pipe

This is the process of squeezing a piping bag in order to force icing or other paste-like mixtures through the tip of the bag for the purpose of decorating or creating special shapes. When piping, different types of nozzles can be used to give different decoration effects.

The most common items of kitchen equipment used in piping are a piping bag and nozzle.

For you to do

4   Look through some recipe books or recipes and write down five different recipes that involve shaping. For each recipe write down what shaping technique is used.

5   There are many different types of piping nozzle that can be used to give different decorative finishes, as can be seen by the celebration cake shown below.

Visit the Imaginative Icing website and write down five different types of nozzle and the type of decoration that each can achieve.

Links to this site and other websites relating to Intermediate 1 Hospitality can be found at the Leckie and Leckie Learning Lab.

LECKIE&LECKIE
Learning Lab

Mix

Mixing is the process of combining ingredients so that they are all distributed evenly within the mixture.

The items of kitchen equipment most commonly used for mixing include fork, spoons, hands, **hand-held electric mixer** and **food processor**.

Whisk

Whisking is the process of using a whisk to blend ingredients together or to incorporate air into ingredients to increase their volume, for example, whisking egg whites.

The most common items of kitchen equipment used for whisking include the **rotary whisk** and the **hand-held electric whisk** for meringues or whisking cream to thicken it.

Cream

Creaming is the process of blending butter and sugar together for the purpose of smoothing the mixture before adding other ingredients to make cake batters, cookie doughs, and bread doughs. When mixed completely, the butter mixture has a light and fluffy texture.

The most common items of kitchen equipment used for creaming are the mixing bowl and wooden spoon. A **hand-held electric whisk** and a **food processor** can also be used for creaming.

For you to do

6 For each of the food preparation techniques listed below, identify the appropriate equipment you would use.

a	peel	f	roll out
b	grate	g	whisk
c	cut	h	mix
d	slice	i	pipe
e	shape	j	cream

The Use of Industrial Equipment

Much of the equipment looked at in this section illustrates the types of equipment that you will find in a typical school kitchen. In professional kitchens, such as those in restaurants, hotels and school dining centres, the types of equipment will be **industrial**. This means that the equipment can process bigger quantities of food and is strong enough to withstand the heavy use it will have in such situations.

Some examples of industrial equipment are given here, along with descriptions of how their use might vary in the industrial kitchen.

Peeling

In an industrial kitchen, peeling potatoes using a potato peeler would be a long and boring task. For this reason there are special pieces of equipment that can be used to speed up this process.

In this type of machine, large quantities of vegetables such as potatoes, carrots and turnips are placed into the machine and peeled. A 25kg bag of potatoes can be peeled in just 4 minutes.

Whisking

In an industrial kitchen, larger more powerful electric whisks are used to cope with the bigger quantities of ingredients that need to be whisked. These whisks are not hand-held but have a sturdy metal base which keeps the machine fixed on the work surface when whisking.

For you to do

7   There are many other items of kitchen equipment that can be used to carry out food preparation tasks. Visit the website of a commercial catering equipment and identify what each of these items of equipment is used for:

a   mandolin

b   French fry cutter

c   sausage stuffer.

Cookery Terms

When reading cookbooks and recipes, it is helpful to know what the **terminology** or special names mean. Some of these terms are in English but some are French in origin, or come from other languages.

Term	Description
Bake blind	To bake without a filling, for example, a pastry case.
Baste	To spoon fat or liquid over food to keep it moist.
Beat	To add a small amount of air to a mixture using a spoon or fork.
Blanch	To dip food ingredients into boiling water for a short time before cooling quickly.
Blend	The process of combining two or more ingredients together, normally a dry and a liquid ingredient, to form a smooth paste, for example, when making a custard or corn flour paste.
Coat	To cover food with, for example, egg and breadcrumbs, to protect it when cooking.
Cream	To mix ingredients together, especially fat and sugar, until they resemble cream (with a light and fluffy texture).
Decorate	To add attractive ingredients to a dish before serving, usually for a sweet dish.
Flake	To divide into small bits.
Fold	To gently mix ingredients together with a metal spoon to prevent air loss.
Garnish	To decorate a savoury dish.
Glaze	To give a shine, usually to baked or roasted foods.
Knead	To gently handle a pastry or dough mixture to give a smooth mixture with no cracks before rolling out or shaping.
Line	To cover the bottom and sides of a flan case with pastry.
Pare	To remove the skin or rind.
Purée	To make a smooth thick paste.
Season	To add salt and pepper.
Strain	To remove solid food from a liquid.
Whip	To beat briskly.
Whisk	The process of using a whisk to combine ingredients together or to incorporate air into ingredients to increase their volume.

Hints and Tips

In your assessment you will be asked to match a range of cookery terms with the correct definitions. The cookery terms and their definitions highlighted opposite in red are the ones that you should know for your assessment. The others are useful terms to know.

For you to do

8 Study each of the pictures below and match each with one of the terms in the table opposite.

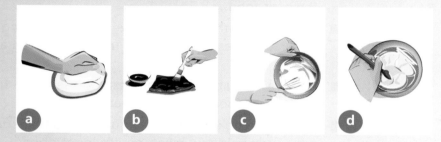

Choose the correct answer to the following questions. If you need help visit the Cookery Online website. Links to this site and other websites relating to Intermediate 1 Hospitality can be found at the Leckie and Leckie Learning Lab.

LECKIE&LECKIE Learning Lab

9 If a recipe says to cook pasta 'al dente', what does this mean literally?

a Until soft	**c** Chew to check texture
b To the teeth	**d** Until chewy

10 What is a bouquet garni?

a A bunch of flowers used to decorate a cake

b A bundle of herbs used to flavour food

c Boiled vegetables

d Chef's apron

11 What is a roux?

a A French chef	**c** A method of cake making
b A method of making a white sauce	**d** A type of fish

12 What is a waffle?

a A method of cooking meat	**c** A bread-like cake
b A cooking pan	**d** A talkative person

13 Find the meaning of the following French cookery terms.

a Brunoise	**c** Flambé
b Mise en place	**d** Chiffonade

Thinking About Food Safety and Hygiene

Kitchen hygiene is hygiene linked to the environment in which food is stored, prepared and cooked (and not to the personal hygiene of the cook or chef).

There are some simple rules that need to be followed to ensure good kitchen hygiene. It is sensible to have a hygienic kitchen, but it is also a **legal requirement** to ensure that all areas where food is being prepared meet hygiene regulations.

Here are a few simple rules.

- Wash chopping boards, dishes, utensils, and work surfaces with hot, soapy water after preparing each food item and before you go on to the next food.
- Wash dish cloths and dish towels in the washing machine with hot water. Sponges should not be used as they can attract and harbour germs.
- Keep raw meat, poultry, and seafood separate from each other and from other foods in the refrigerator.
- Never put cooked food on an unwashed plate or chopping board that previously held raw meat, poultry or seafood.
- Refrigerate or freeze perishables, prepared foods and leftovers within 2 hours of a meal.
- Defrost frozen foods in the refrigerator or under cold running water, not on the work surface.
- Dispose of all waste correctly in bins with well-fitting lids.
- All food premises must have separate facilities for washing hands and for food preparation.
- Food preparation areas should be well ventilated and have good lighting.
- Food should always be covered to prevent contamination.
- Clean as you go – wipe up spills immediately and clean equipment after use.
- Animals must not be allowed in food preparation areas.

Cleaning

Cleaning is an important part of the maintenance of all food businesses. Clean premises, work surfaces and equipment help to maintain good food safety and hygiene.

Why do we clean?

- Because the law states that food premises must be clean.
- To prevent food poisoning or food contamination.
- To avoid prosecution.
- To keep customers.
- To keep equipment working properly.

There are important terms that you need to know about cleaning:

- **disinfection** – reducing bacteria to a safe level
- **disinfectant** – a chemical used to disinfect surfaces
- **detergent** – a chemical used to remove dirt from surfaces.

Cleaning involves the use of detergents to remove dirt and the use of disinfectants to reduce bacteria to safe minimum levels.

There are two main methods of cleaning crockery and dishes in a food premises:

- machine/dishwasher method – using a dishwasher to clean equipment and dishes
- two-sink method – one sink for disinfecting and one for rinsing.

In general the following procedures should be followed when cleaning:

1 pre clean – removing leftover food and residues
2 main clean – cleaning using hot water and detergent
3 rinse – with clean hot water to remove detergent
4 disinfect – to kill bacteria using a food-safe disinfectant
5 final rinse – to remove any disinfectant
6 dry – to remove all moisture.

For you to do

14 How often do you think each of the following areas should be cleaned?
  a food preparation surfaces for raw foods
  b food preparation surfaces for cooked foods
  c chef's knives
  d kitchen floors
  e kitchen windows
  f waste bins

A Quick Word About Smoking

Recent legislation in Scotland has brought about a ban on smoking in all enclosed buildings. This includes pubs, restaurants and hotels. Smoking is never allowed in a food preparation area because of the possibility of contaminating food either by cigarette ash falling into food or by germs passing from the mouth to food via the hand holding a cigarette.

No smoking
It is against the law to smoke in this restaurant

Classification of Methods of Heat Transfer and Cooking Mediums

Humans are the only creatures on Earth that cook food to eat, and it is thought that we started to cook food by accident. Over many centuries we have developed very stylish methods of preparing and cooking foods.

Why do we cook food? We cook food for many reasons:

- to improve the texture of food
- to improve the flavour of food
- to kill bacteria and so make food safer to eat
- to make food easier to digest.

Cooking food involves applying heat to it. Heating food causes chemical changes in the food, resulting in changes to its structure, appearance and flavour.

So how does heat get to the food? This depends on the method of cooking being used. Different methods of cooking heat food in different ways. In order to understand this better, you need know about **heat transfer**, the way in which heat can travel into food.

Heat transfer happens in three main ways:

- conduction
- convection
- radiation.

Conduction

Conduction is the process of transferring heat through a hot solid surface directly on to a cold solid surface. Heat is a form of energy, and always travels from a point of higher energy to a point of lower energy, that is from a warmer to a cooler surface. Conduction also takes place in liquids. This is why water, for example, is used for many cooking processes, such as boiling.

An example of conduction is frying a steak in a frying pan.

In this example heat travels from the burner or cooker ring to the pan, heating up the pan. When the steak is added to the pan, heat travels from the warmed pan to the steak, heating (cooking) it.

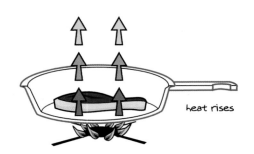

heat rises

Metals are good **conductors** of heat and this is why they are used for cooking pots. Plastics and wood are not good conductors of heat and this is why they are used for parts of equipment that you don't want to heat up, such as pan handles. (Hot pan handles make it difficult to hold the pan.)

Convection

Convection is the process of transferring heat either through liquid, such as water or stock, or through air.

Hot water or air always rises, replacing cooler water or air. This causes a constant movement or **circulation** of hot liquid or air. This movement is called a **convection current**.

Two different examples of convection cooking are boiling potatoes and roasting beef.

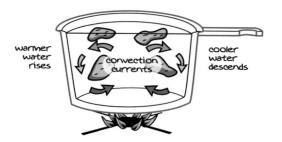

When boiling potatoes, the boiling water circulates around the potatoes, transferring heat and causing them to cook.

When roasting beef, the air in the oven circulates around the beef, transferring heat and causing it to cook.

Radiation

This is the direct transfer of heat on to the surface of food via radiation. The term 'radiation' isn't scary, and doesn't just refer to energy generated by a nuclear processing plant or used in X-ray machines. There are many different types of radiation, for example, grilling uses radiated heat that does not emit dangerous radiation rays.

Conductor: *an item that allows heat to travel through it easily.*
Circulate: *to move in a circular motion.*

An example of radiation is grilling bacon.

When grilling bacon the powerful heat from the grill falls directly on to the surface of the bacon, causing it to cook. The heat source falls only on one side of the food, so the food needs to be turned regularly to ensure even and full cooking.

When cooking foods, different types of heat transfer take place. Within most cookery processes, there will be different types of heat transfer taking place at the one time. There is usually a **main source** of heat transfer as well as a **secondary source** of heat transfer. For example, when boiling eggs we use both conduction and convection.

For you to do

1 Look at the diagram below which shows a cake cooking in an oven. The cake is in a metal baking tin.

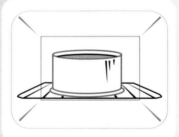

a What are the main types of heat transfer taking place?
b Draw a simple diagram to show the direction of the heat transfer.

Cooking Mediums

Usually when we cook food, we cook using a **cooking medium**. A cooking medium is a liquid that is used to assist in the transfer of heat, such as oil, water, stock or steam. Different cooking methods use different cooking mediums. These are discussed in more detail later in this chapter (see pages 52–65).

Classification of Cooking Methods

Methods of cooking are **classified** (grouped together) according to the cooking medium that is needed for heat transfer. There are two main classifications:

- wet methods of cooking
- dry methods of cooking.

Wet methods of cooking require the use of a liquid in which the food will be cooked. Wet methods include: boiling, steaming, poaching, stewing and casseroling.

Dry methods of cooking do not require the use of a liquid. Dry methods include: grilling, baking, shallow frying and barbecuing.

Hints and Tips

You might think that shallow frying should be classified as a wet method of cooking. However, frying is classified as a dry method because the food is submerged or placed in fat or oil that does not contain water.

Boiling

Description

Boiling is a method of cooking in which prepared food is cooked in a liquid, for example, water or stock.

The boiling action can be either:

- quick and **vigorous**, for example, when boiling potatoes (generally the cooking medium is at boiling point)
- slow and gentle, for example, when simmering a stew (generally the cooking medium is at a temperature just below boiling point).

Vigorous: *strong, forceful.*

Boiling is classified a **wet** method of cooking. The cooking **medium** is generally **water** but it can also be stock, flavoured water or wine.

Heat transfer

- Conduction by the action of heat from the burner or cooker ring transferring through the pot to heat the water and food.
- Convection by the movement of hot water surrounding the food.
- Conduction of heat through the food.

Suitable foods

The following foods are suitable for boiling:

- meat and poultry, particularly for tougher cuts of meat that require long cooking times
- fish and shellfish, for example, lobster
- eggs
- pasta and rice
- fresh and frozen vegetables, for example, turnips, potatoes, parsnips, carrots and peas.

Hints and Tips

Fruit such as tomatoes and peaches can be placed into boiling water for 10 seconds and then plunged into cold water to loosen the skin. They are then easier to peel.

Cooking appliances

Pots and pans are usually used for boiling. Domestic pots and pans that are used in the home are slightly different from those used in a commercial or industrial kitchen where they need to cater for larger quantities.

Additional information

■ Food can be added to either cold liquid prior to being heated to boiling point, or directly added to boiling liquid.

■ Cold liquid is used when a clear liquid is needed or where safety is an issue.

■ Boiling water is used to keep cooking times short and so help to reduce loss of nutrients and colour.

A Bratt pan is an industrial cooking appliance that is used to produce large quantities of cooked food. A Bratt pan can be used for boiling, shallow frying, stewing and general cooking.

Hints and Tips

You cannot boil fish. If you try to boil fish, the fish flesh would break up into small pieces. You can boil shellfish, though, for example, lobster.

Do not over-cook vegetables. Over-cooking causes important vitamins to be lost as well as harming the vegetables' colour, texture and flavour.

Tips for healthy eating

✔ Always add potatoes to boiling water, and only use just enough water to cover the potatoes in order to minimise loss of nutrients during cooking.

For you to do

2 Find out how long it takes to boil four servings of the following foods:

a   cabbage   e   egg noodles
b   broccoli   f   boiled pasta
c   carrots   g   fresh pasta
d   rice   h   potatoes

3 Using recipe books or the internet, find out how to cook a live lobster.

In your answer explain the cooking time, the cooking method and your thoughts on this cooking method.

Stewing

Description

Stewing is a method of cooking in which prepared food such as diced meat is cooked in a minimal (small) amount of cooking liquid. Both the food and the liquid in which the food is cooked are served. Stewing is a good method of cooking for tougher cuts of meat and poultry which require a longer, slower and more gentle cooking process. Serving the liquid with the food also means that any nutrients that have seeped or leaked from the food into the liquid will not be lost.

Fruit can also be stewed or cooked slowly to a **pulp**, for example, stewed rhubarb.

Stewing is classified a **wet** method of cooking. The cooking **medium** is generally **water** but it can also be stock, flavoured water or wine.

Heat transfer

- Conduction by the action of heat from the burner or cooker ring transferring through the pot to heat the water and food.
- Convection by the movement of hot water surrounding the food.
- Conduction of heat through the food.

Suitable foods

The following foods are suitable for stewing:

- fish and shellfish
- red and white meat – generally the tougher cuts of beef, mutton, lamb, **veal** and pork
- poultry and game
- vegetables, for example, vegetables cooked in a **ratatouille**
- fruit such as apples, pears and rhubarb which are generally cooked until they form a soft pulp, losing their shape.

Cooking appliances

Stewing is generally done using pots and pans with tight fitting lids. Domestic pots and pans that are used in the home are slightly different to those used in a commercial or industrial kitchen.

Hints and Tips

When stewing foods, monitoring the cooking process is very important as the cooking temperature should be just below boiling point. You should see small bubbles just bursting through the cooking liquid.

Additional information

- Stewing is the name given to this process when a pan and kitchen hob are used. **Casseroling** is the name used when the cooking is started on the hob but completed in the oven.

- There are generally two different types of stews:
  - *brown stew* – where the end product is brown in colour, for example, beef stew
  - *white stew* – where the end product is white or blond in colour, for example, chicken **fricassée**.

- Stews need to be monitored regularly to make sure there is enough liquid in the stew, and also to check that the food is not sticking to the bottom of the pan.

- Many stews require long cooking times – you need to take this into account when developing a work plan.

> **Pulp:** *a soft, wet mass of cooked fruit.*
> **Veal:** *meat from a calf which is identifiable by its pale colour.*
> **Ratatouille:** *a savoury dish made by cooking vegetables such as tomatoes and courgettes in a liquid over a slow heat.*
> **Fricassée:** *a dish made of pieces of meat especially chicken or veal, cooked and served in a white sauce.*

For you to do

4 Find three recipes that use stewing as a cookery process.
- One recipe must be a starter.
- One recipe must be a savoury dish.
- One recipe must be a sweet dish.

For each recipe, note the recipe name, the ingredients that are being stewed and the total cooking time.

Poaching

Description

Poaching is a method of cooking in which prepared food is cooked in a liquid. The food is cooked at temperatures below boiling point (usually 73–93°C) where there is little or no movement from the cooking liquid. Poaching is generally used for delicate foods that need gentle cooking. Poaching is classified a **wet** method of cooking. The cooking **medium** is generally **water** but it can also be stock, milk or wine.

Heat transfer

- Conduction by the action of heat from the burner or cooker ring transferring through the pot to heat the water and food.
- Convection by the movement of hot water or steam surrounding the food.
- Conduction of heat through the food.

Suitable foods

The following foods are suitable for poaching:

- fish, including shellfish
- whole chicken
- eggs
- fresh and dried fruits, such as pears and peaches.

Cooking appliances

Appliances used in poaching are pots and pans, including saucepans, shallow-sided pots and fish kettles (a fish kettle is specially designed for poaching whole fish).

Additional information

- There are two types of poaching:
  - *deep poaching* – where food is fully covered in the minimum amount of liquid and gently cooked. In most cases the food is placed into the hot liquid, for example, whole fish
  - *shallow poaching* – where the food is partly covered with liquid and cooked gently under cover in an oven, for example, small items of food such as cuts of fish and poultry.
- It is important to ensure that food is being poached and not boiled so regular monitoring is important.
- Food items that are poached will retain their shape better, due to the gentle nature of the cooking (unlike in stewing).

Hints and Tips

Poached eggs are often cooked and kept chilled in iced water. When required for serving they are then reheated.

For you to do

5 For each statement below, identify whether it is:

- ■ an advantage of poaching (A)
- ■ a disadvantage of poaching (D)
- ■ not related to poaching (NR).

a   Food is easily digested when poached.

b   Skill is required when poaching.

c   Poaching is not a suitable cooking method for all foods.

d   It is an inexpensive method of heat transfer.

e   The food item needs to be brushed with oils before cooking.

f   Suitable for large cuts of meat and poultry.

6 *Blockbuster!* Name five foods that are suitable for poaching. Each food must start with the letter A, B, C, D or E (aim for one of each).

Steaming

Description

Steaming is a method of cooking where prepared food is cooked in steam. The water is heated to 100°C or above (under pressure) to produce steam. The steam may either come into direct contact with the food or the food may be protected in a container and it is the container which the steam heats and which cooks the food. Steaming is classified a **wet** method of cooking. The cooking **medium** is usually **water**.

Heat transfer

- Conduction by the action of heat from the burner or cooker ring transferring through the pot to heat the water and food.
- Convection by the movement of steam surrounding the food.
- Conduction of heat through the food and/or container.

Suitable foods

The following foods are suitable for steaming:

- eggs
- fish and shellfish
- vegetables, including potatoes
- savoury and sweet puddings, for example, steamed sponge.

Cooking appliances

There are different items of equipment that can be used for steaming, depending on the situation:

Saucepan – a small amount of water is placed in a saucepan and the food is put into a wire basket above the water line. A tight fitting lid is placed on top. Special steaming saucepans can be purchased.

Commercial steamers are used in commercial kitchens to cook larger amounts of food quickly and at higher temperatures than could be achieved using the saucepan method.

Additional information

- Care needs to be taken when using commercial steamers as they can generate high temperatures.
- Steaming is a gentle process and care needs to be taken not to over-cook foods.
- Many high street electrical stores sell electric steamers specifically designed for use in the home.

Hints and Tips

Steaming vegetables is a healthy method of cooking because you do not need to add fat and there is little loss of nutrients because the food is not immersed in water.

For you to do

7 Complete the word search on steaming on the Leckie and Leckie website. Go to: www.leckieandleckie.co.uk, click on the Learning Lab button and navigate to the Intermediate 1 Hospitality Course Notes page.

LECKIE&LECKIE
Learning Lab

Hints and Tips

When steaming an egg, remember to cool it immediately in cold water to prevent the area between the yolk and white becoming discoloured. And did you know you can steam frozen vegetables from a frozen state?

Baking

Description

Baking is a method of cooking in which prepared food and food products are cooked in a **pre-heated** oven. Most baked foods are cooked in a container to allow them to maintain the required shape. Baking can generally be used for many types of food, although its main use is in **confectionery**, pastry and bakery items. Baking is classified a **dry** method of cooking. There is generally **no cooking medium**.

Heat transfer

- Conduction through the pan and the oven shelf.
- Convection from the hot air which is circulating in the oven.

Suitable foods

The following foods are suitable for baking:

- fruits, for example, apples and pears
- potatoes
- milk and egg custard puddings, for example, baked rice
- flour products, for example, cakes and biscuits
- meat and vegetable **hotpots**
- eggs.

Cooking appliances

In the home the cooking appliance is usually either a gas or electric oven.

In a commercial kitchen there are specialist baking cookers such as pastry ovens, and some specialist ovens such as pizza ovens.

Additional information

- When baking, it is important that ovens are pre-heated to the correct cooking temperature.
- Accurate weighing and measuring is important when preparing ingredients for baking.

Pre-heated: *warmed to the correct temperature before the items to be cooked are placed in the oven.*
Confectionery: *sweets or chocolate.*
Hotpot: *a mixture of meats and vegetables usually including sliced potatoes, cooked slowly in a covered dish.*

Hints and Tips

When baking bread, a brown crust forms and this is usually a sign that the bread is ready. However, it is important to remember to test the food for readiness. See page 68 for more information.

For you to do

8 Find out the meaning of the following words or terms, all of which are used in professional kitchens and relate to baking:

    a batch cooking

    b provers

    c bloom

    d coating

    e shortening

    f resting.

9 *Blockbuster!* Name five foods that are suitable for baking. Each food must start with the letter A, F, G, N and P.

Hints and Tips

When baking pastry, allow it to rest before cooking. This will prevent it from shrinking in the oven. When writing a time plan, remember to include resting time if needed.

Tips for healthy eating

✔ Pastry can be high in fat, particularly puff and flaky pastry.

✔ Meringues are very high in sugar.

Grilling

Description

Grilling is a quick method of cooking in which prepared food is cooked, mainly with very **intense** and direct heat from the heat source, for example, an electric grill, gas grill or flames from a barbecue. The heat may be directly above and/or below the food being cooked. This quick method of cooking helps to retain nutrients. Grilling is not suitable for either tougher cuts of meat that require long slow methods of cookery or for very thick cuts of meat. Grilling is classified a **dry** method of cooking. There is **no cooking medium** required.

Heat transfer

- Radiated heat directly onto the surface of the food.
- Conducted heat from the wire bars or surface of the grill.
- Conduction through the food.

Suitable foods

The following foods are suitable for grilling:

- good quality cuts of meats, for example, steak, shops, cutlets
- bacon and offal, for example, liver
- poultry and game
- fish and shellfish
- vegetables, for example, mushrooms and tomatoes
- other meat and meat-substitute products such as burgers and sausages.

Hints and Tips

Certain cuts of meat such as steak and chicken and also some vegetables such as peppers and aubergine can be cut into cubes and threaded onto skewers to make kebabs.

Grilling mushrooms? If you are using bought mushrooms do not peel them. If you are using field mushrooms, peel before using. Brush the mushrooms lightly with vegetable oil before grilling and this will prevent them from drying out.

Tips for healthy eating

✔ *Making seafish skewers?* Sprinkle with wholemeal breadcrumbs before cooking. Not only does this protect the delicate flesh when grilling, but it also adds fibre.

Cooking appliances

- Domestic gas or electric grills are most commonly used.
- Steak grills and barbecue grills fired by **charcoal**, gas or electricity are also used.

Industrial appliances include:

- *salamander grill* – a grill used for overhead grilling of steaks, fish, sausages, etc. It can also be used for **flash heating** and browning of dishes prior to serving

- *contact grill* – a grill used for grilling over and under the food item at the same time. It grills evenly on both sides and is available with different grill plates, for example, ribbed plates or panini plates.

Additional information

- Food to be grilled is usually lightly brushed with oil prior to cooking. This prevents the surface of the food from drying out.
- Grilling can be used to sear or brown foods to give colour and flavour.
- Most grilled foods need to be turned during cooking so that they cook evenly.

> Intense: *extremely forceful or strong.*
> Charcoal: *a hard black substance similar to coal that can be use for cooking.*
> Flash heating: *to heat something quickly.*

For you to do

10 Visit the website of Meat Matters and find information to answer the following questions.

   a Why might grilling be regarded as a 'low fat' method of cooking?

   b How far should you position the grill pan from the heat source when grilling a steak?

   c How long should a lamb chop be grilled on each side?

   d What factors might affect this cooking time?

   e Name two different types of sauces that are recommended for serving with steak.

Links to this website and other websites relating to Intermediate 1 Hospitality can be found at: www.leckieandleckie.co.uk, clicking on the Learning Lab button and navigating to the Intermediate 1 Hospitality Course Notes page.

LECKIE&LECKIE
Learning Lab

Shallow Frying

Description

Shallow frying is a method of cooking where prepared food is cooked in a pre-heated pan or a metal surface with a small amount of fat or oil. Shallow frying is a fast method of cooking and is suitable only for certain foods that can be cooked quickly. Shallow frying is classified a **dry** method of cooking. The cooking **medium** is **oil** or **fat**.

Heat transfer

- Conduction from the heat source to the pan.
- Conduction of heat through the food.

Suitable foods

The following foods are suitable for shallow frying:

- meats such as steaks, chops, cutlets
- offal and bacon
- poultry
- fish
- eggs, for example, fried eggs and omelettes
- vegetables, for example, onions and mushrooms
- fruits, for example, bananas, apples and pineapple
- batters and dough, for example, crêpes, scones and pancakes.

Cooking appliances

Cooking appliances include standard frying pans but also more specialist pans, for example:

omelette pan   *sauté pan*   *sauteuse pan*   *wok*

- *omelette pan* – specially shaped pan with curved sides for cooking an omelette
- *sauté pan* – pan with straight vertical sides and used for shallow frying of meat and potatoes
- *sauteuse pan* – pan with sloping sides used for **reducing** sauces
- *wok* – Chinese pan used for fast frying food, for example, stir frying.

Additional information

- Foods which are shallow fried need to be carefully turned to ensure even cooking.

- Shallow frying can be used to sear foods, that is, cooking the food in very hot oil to seal in the juices and flavour and to develop a brown colour.

- There are many different forms of frying:

  -  *meunière* – shallow frying of fish and shellfish

  - *sauter* – usually means to shallow fry and use a tossing action when turning the food, but is also used as a general term for shallow frying small cuts of meat, or to mean the preparation of a quality meat dish with sauce

  - *griddle* – to cook items on a lightly oiled, ridged metal plate, called a griddle

  - *stir fry* – to cook fish, meats or vegetables quickly in oil

  - *sweat* – to fry items slowly in a little fat, using a lid and without allowing the food to develop a colour. This is usually a preparation stage in making other items, such as soup.

> **Reduce:** *to thicken a sauce by boiling it, making the flavour stronger and decreasing its volume.*

Hints and Tips

If you are shallow frying fish, cook the skin side first. This will make the skin crispy and since this is the side that will be uppermost when served on the plate – called the presentation side – it will look appealing.

Serving fried eggs with a soft yolk may cause food poisoning.

Shallow frying food at too low a temperature will result in the food absorbing fat so making it greasy.

Tips for healthy eating

- ✔ Cooking steak? Try using a non-stick pan polished with oil. This reduces the fat content of the dish.

- ✔ Shallow-fried breaded items are high in fat. Try using wholemeal breadcrumbs rather than white, as this increases fibre content.

For you to do

11 You have been asked to prepare a fillet of haddock for frying. The chef has asked you to 'bread' the fish to protect it when being fried.

List the ingredients that you would need to bread a fillet of haddock and briefly describe the use of each ingredient.

Testing for Readiness

An important part of a chef's job is to know when food is ready following cooking. This comes with experience and there are tools that can help you, such as a temperature probe. However, there are a number of characteristics that you can look for in a food product that will let you know if the food is cooked adequately and ready for serving.

The following techniques describe how you can test to check if food is ready for serving.

Root Vegetables

Root vegetables such as potatoes, onions and turnips (but not carrots) should feel soft when firm pressure is applied. If you can easily pierce a vegetable with a fork (you don't have to force the fork), then the vegetable is cooked.

Other Vegetables

Vegetables that grow above ground, such as beans, broccoli and cauliflower, should have a crisp but tender texture when ready. The vegetable should resist being pierced with a fork.

Steak

Some grilled or fried foods must be cooked to the correct degree in order to meet customer wishes. Steak is an example. When you order a steak in a restaurant you are often asked how you would like it cooked. The following chart provides information about degrees of cooking.

Cookery term	Translation	Description
Au bleu	Very rare	Sealed for a few seconds only on each side. The meat looks nearly raw.
Saignant	Bleeding	The cooked meat has a reddish **tinge** – it is underdone or rare.
A point	Just done or medium	The meat has a slight pinkness.
Bien cuit	Well cooked	The meat is thoroughly cooked, and there is no pink colour.

Poultry

The skin covering the flesh should be dark gold in colour. Use a skewer to prick the thigh of the chicken; when the juices run clear and not pink, the chicken is cooked.

Fish

Fish is cooked the moment that the tip of a thin-bladed knife passes easily through the thickest part. You can also do what is called a **sight test**. If the flesh under the skin is **translucent** then the fish is not ready. If the flesh is **opaque,** it is cooked. Another test is that the flesh of the fish should 'flake' or come away from the bone of the fish easily.

Pasta

When boiling pasta test for readiness by removing a piece from the water and tasting it. (Check it every 30 seconds after the minimum suggested cooking time has passed.) When ready, pasta should look slightly swollen with water and feel tender in your mouth, yet have a little 'bite' or substance to it. This is known as 'al dente'. If the water in which the pasta is becoming cloudy, then you are over-cooking the pasta.

Rice

When boiling rice test for readiness by removing a grain from the pan and tasting. It should feel soft with no hard or grainy parts within it. You can test this also by squeezing a grain between your fingers – again it should not feel grainy. You can also tell by looking at the rice – it should look swollen, but not 'burst'.

Whipping cream and egg whites

It is easy to over-whisk cream – and if you do, it turns into what looks like butter. Test the cream as you whisk it. Lift the whisk straight up out of the bowl. If the cream is ready, then it should rise up in a little peak, with the tip flipped over. This is referred to as **soft peak** stage. The same method applies when whisking egg whites. If the recipe calls for **stiff peaks** you should whisk for a little longer until the peak does not flip over.

> **Tinge:** *a very slight amount of colour.*
> **Translucent:** *almost transparent, see-through.*
> **Opaque:** *not transparent or see-through.*
> **Resist:** *to fight against or block something.*
> **Puncture:** *to make a small hole in something.*

Cakes

These should be golden brown in colour. Gently press the top of the sponge with your fingertips – it should feel slightly spongy to touch. Alternatively, take a cocktail stick and pass it through the cake at the deepest part. If the cocktail stick comes out clean, the cake is ready. If the cake is in a cake tin you should see that there is a slight space between the edge of the cake and the cake tin – as if it has shrunk.

Bread

Baked breads should be golden brown in colour. Once the bread has been removed from the oven, gently tap the underside of the bread. If it sounds 'hollow' it is ready. Alternatively, take a skewer and pass it through the bread at the deepest part. If the skewer comes out clean, the bread is ready.

Thinking About Hygiene and Food Safety

The Importance of Temperature

It is important in cookery to use the correct temperature, to make sure that food is safe to eat. This is important during all stages of food production and cooking.

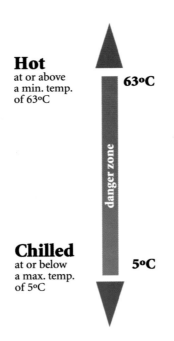

Hot
at or above
a min. temp.
of 63ºC

63ºC

danger zone

Chilled
at or below
a max. temp.
of 5ºC

5ºC

The Food Safety Act 1990 and the Food Hygiene (Scotland) Regulations 2006 make specific references to temperature and provide specific guidance to all those involved in food production. These regulations state that foods which need to be controlled by temperature to ensure safety must be held either **hot** or **chilled**.

This means that foods which need to be stored or held at low temperatures until sold/served should be placed into a refrigerator, refrigerating chamber or cool ventilated place.

It also means that food which is being **held hot** to be served should be maintained at a temperature of **at least 63°C**.

If foods are being **reheated**, then the food has to reach a temperature of **at least 82°C**.

Bacteria and other micro-organisms that can cause food poisoning are able to multiply rapidly at temperatures of 5–63°C. This is why the regulations state specific temperatures.

Safety When Cooking

It is important that all food preparation staff are aware of the procedures if there is a fire in the kitchen, particularly a fire caused by a frying pan catching fire.

Where a pan fire happens the following steps should be followed:

Always

- Act in a safe manner.
- Turn off the ring or burner or frying equipment.
- Turn off at the mains.
- Place a fire blanket over the fire.
- Tell the supervisor.
- If necessary sound the fire alarm.

Never

- Allow the oil or fat to over-heat.
- Leave frying pans unattended.
- Over-fill a frying pan.
- Use water to put out a frying pan fire.

Note: electric frying pans should be serviced on a regular basis.

For you to do

12 a What temperature should a ready-made trifle in a supermarket be stored at?

b What temperature should a hot pie in a takeaway café reach?

c What temperature should a chicken curry that is being reheated for sale at lunchtime in a canteen reach?

d What temperature should fresh fish from a supermarket be stored at?

e What temperature should a pot of beans in a supermarket café reach?

f What temperature should a bottle of milk be stored at?

g What temperature should left-over roast beef in gravy that has been held in a refrigerator overnight reach?

Food Hygiene

Tiny micro-organisms such as bacteria are all around us – in the air we breathe, on work surfaces and on our food. Many of these micro-organisms are safe and will cause us no harm, but others can cause illness, such as **food poisoning**. We can control those micro-organisms that cause food poisoning, usually by by heating (cooking) and/or chilling (refrigerating) our food, but given the chance they can easily spread around the kitchen – via our hands, chopping boards, cloths, knives and other utensils, and even our clothes. Good kitchen hygiene and good personal hygiene are important to help control the spread of harmful germs. Good food hygiene is all about controlling harmful bacteria which can cause serious illness.

Good hygiene

- is essential for you to make or sell food that is safe to eat
- helps you obey the law
- reduces the risk of food poisoning among your customers
- helps protect your business's reputation.

Poor hygiene

- could lead to prosecution or legal action, especially if a customer becomes ill
- may cause loss of customers
- may affect reputation badly.

Key terms

Food hygiene: practices that prevent contamination of food, ensuring that food is acceptable and safe to eat.

Food poisoning: an illness caused by eating contaminated food.

Food contamination: the infection or spoilage of food by foreign bodies, making the food unacceptable or harmful to eat.

Food spoilage: the process of a food being changed or damaged so as to make it unsafe or undesirable to eat.

Pathogenic bacteria: bacteria that cause disease or illness.

Toxins: poisons produced by some micro-organisms that can cause illness.

Food-borne infection: an illness caused by eating food which is infected by micro-organisms.

Food Poisoning

Many people have probably suffered from food poisoning but not realised it, thinking that their upset stomach or diarrhoea is caused by a 'bug going around' rather than food poisoning. A report by the Consumers' Association estimated that as many as 4.5 million cases of food poisoning go unreported each year in the UK. (Source: *The Scotsman*, January 2002.)

The symptoms of food poisoning vary depending on the type of bacteria that has caused the illness, but include:

- diarrhoea
- stomach ache
- vomiting
- fever
- nausea
- headache
- dizziness

You would generally not have all of these symptoms at one time.

There are many causes of food poisoning:

- preparing foods too far in advance
- not cooking foods properly
- not defrosting foods correctly
- storing foods incorrectly (i.e. too warm) so that bacteria can grow quickly
- cross-contamination of foods after cooking
- food handlers infecting food.

Everybody is at risk of infection from poor food hygiene, but some are more at risk than others. The elderly and the young, pregnant women, and those who are recovering from illness generally have greater difficulty fighting illness caused by food poisoning.

Effective hygiene can be achieved by following good personal and kitchen hygiene rules.

- **Personal hygiene** is hygiene relating to the individual – the food worker.
- **Kitchen hygiene** is hygiene relating to the kitchen environment (see pages 88–91).

Contamination of Food by Micro-organisms

This section deals with food contaminated by micro-organisms; other ways of contaminating food are described on page 79.

Micro-organisms

There are four main types of micro-organisms:

- bacteria
- moulds
- yeasts
- viruses.

Bacteria

Bacteria are very small, single-celled organisms that we cannot see, but they are all around us. Some are good for us, essential for good health. Other bacteria are used by food manufacturers to make cheese and yoghurt, for example. However, some bacteria are bad for us, and can cause illness if enough of the bacteria get into our bodies. These are known as **pathogenic bacteria**. Different types of bacteria and the illnesses they cause are described on pages 76–77.

Moulds

Moulds are also single-celled organisms that branch together, providing a furry or fluffy appearance on foods, for example, on bread and jam. Sometimes food manufacturers use moulds in the manufacturing process. For example, moulds are added to some cheeses during the cheese-making process to improve flavour.

For you to do

1 Your teacher will provide you with some examples of cheeses that have had mould added during manufacture. Write down the names of the different types of cheese and what they look like.
Can you see the mould? Try them if you want!
Did you like each type of cheese? Explain why or why not.

Yeasts

Yeasts are also single-celled organisms commonly found in the soil and on our skin. They are bigger than bacteria. Yeasts can cause food to spoil and can also cause illnesses, such as skin infections. However, not all yeasts are harmful, for example, yeasts are used in the production of bread and alcohol.

Viruses

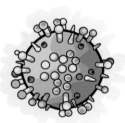

Viruses are very small micro-organisms, much smaller than bacteria. They can cause illnesses, such as viral food poisoning. They get into the body through contaminated food, and then they grow and multiply inside the living cells of the body.

For you to do

2 Research the use of yeasts, moulds and bacteria in the manufacture of foods and drinks. Find some examples of each.
Are there any that really surprise you?
Do they put you off consuming that food or drink?

Conditions for Growth of Bacteria

In many cases you need a large number of bacteria to be present in the body before they cause illness. Bacteria grow and multiply quickly in certain conditions. They need:

- warmth
- moisture
- time
- food
- air
- a suitable pH.

Warmth

Bacteria need to be warm in order to grow and multiply. As you can see from the temperature guide, at some temperatures (between 5°C and 63°C) bacteria will grow quickly. At lower temperatures (lower than 5°C) growth of bacteria slows down completely, until the bacteria become **dormant** (go to sleep). At higher temperatures (above 63°C) bacteria begin to die.

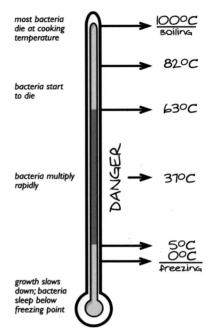

For you to do

3 Answer these questions, using the diagram of the thermometer for reference.

   a Between which temperature range will bacteria grow most quickly?

   b At what temperature will bacteria begin to die?

   c At what temperature does bacterial growth begin to slow down?

   d At what temperature do bacteria become dormant?

Moisture

Bacteria need moisture to survive. They cannot grow where there is no moisture.

Time

Bacteria need time to grow. One single bacterium can divide into two in just 20 minutes. So in the space of a few hours, thousands of bacteria can be present.

Food

Bacteria also need food to grow. Bacteria prefer foods that have a high water content and are usually rich in protein. These foods are generally called **high-risk foods** and include:

- meat and meat products
- poultry
- eggs
- milk
- seafood
- cooked rice.

Foods that need to be refrigerated or which are classified as **perishable** foods are often ideal for bacterial growth.

Perishable: *spoils quickly.*

Air

Most bacteria require oxygen to grow. These are known as **aerobic** bacteria. However, some bacteria can grow without the need for air. These are known as **anaerobic** bacteria.

pH

pH is the measure of how acidic or alkaline a substance is:

- a pH of 0–6 is **acidic**
- a pH of 7 is **neutral**
- a pH of 8–14 is **alkaline**.

In general bacteria cannot grow in conditions that are too acidic or too alkaline. Most bacteria prefer a pH of 7, which is neutral (and is the pH of pure water).

For you to do

4 Which of the following foods would be classified as high-risk foods?
- **a** individual steak pie
- **b** chicken
- **c** bar of chocolate
- **d** pear
- **e** Chinese rice-based takeaway food
- **f** potato
- **g** fish
- **h** peanuts

Bacteria that Cause Food Poisoning

This table lists the main types of bacteria that cause food poisoning that you might come across in your course of work.

Bacteria	Source	Likely foods
Salmonella	Raw meat, milk, egg, carriers, pets, rodents, water, sewage	Contaminated high-risk foods which require no further preparation or treatment
Clostridium perfringens	Animal and human faeces, dust, soil, raw meat and insects	Large quantities of high-risk food such as gravy, sauces, stews, lasagne, meat dishes, joints
Staphylococcus aureus	Human nose, skin, boils, cuts, mouth	High-risk foods (as above)
Clostridium botulinum	Soil, fish, meat and vegetables	Canned foods, smoked fish
Bacillus cereus	Cereals, rice, dust and soil	Cooked rice
E.coli 0157	Sewage, water and raw meat	Contaminated cooked products, unwashed infected salad items
Campylobacter	Raw poultry and meat, unpasteurised milk, untreated water	Raw or undercooked meat or poultry, food infected by animal faeces
Listeria	Soil, water, domestic animals and human faeces	Contaminated meat products, pâté, seafood, poultry, vegetables, cook chill products, soft cheeses, prepared salads
Dysentery	Faeces of infected people, flies, cockroaches	Salads, unpeeled fruits, ice cream and ice cubes
Typhoid	Water or food contaminated by faeces or urine	Infected food or water

Incubation: *period of time from beginning of infection to appearance of symptoms.*

Incubation	Duration of illness	Symptoms
6–72 hours; more often 12–36 hours	1–7 days (may be longer)	Diarrhoea, vomiting, fever, abdominal pain. May lead to infection such as blood poisoning and ultimately death.
8–22 hours, more often 12–18 hours	Approx. 12–48 hours	Abdominal pain, diarrhoea.
1–6 hours	6–24 hours	Abdominal pain, vomiting, high temperature.
2 hours to 8 days; more often 12–36 hours	Long-term (months)	May lead to death following paralysis of the nervous and respiratory system.
1–5 hours or 8–16 hours	12–48 hours	Vomiting and/or diarrhoea.
10–72 hours; more often 12–24 hours	Up to 5 days	Abdominal pain, diarrhoea, vomiting. May lead to infection and kidney failure.
2–5 days, sometimes longer	Maximum of 7 days	Fever, headache, abdominal pain and diarrhoea.
3 days to 3 weeks	Varies	Fever, headaches, nausea, sickness. Can damage the unborn child.
1–7 days	Varies	Diarrhoea, fever, cramps, vomiting.
1–21 days	Can last several weeks	Headache, loss of appetite, tiredness constipation. May be followed by fever, stomach pain and diarrhoea.

Cross-contamination

It is very easy to pass micro-organisms from person to person, from person to equipment and from person to food. This is called **cross-contamination**.

There are two different types of contamination:

- **direct cross-contamination:** this is where there is direct contact between the contaminant and the cooked food during storage, preparation, cooking or serving.

- **indirect cross-contamination:** this is where food becomes contaminated because it is in contact with something else that has been in contact with contaminated food, for example, the transfer of bacteria from raw to cooked food by the use of the same unwashed cooks knife.

For you to do

5 Answer these questions, using the bacteria chart on pages 76–77 for reference.

    a Why shouldn't a pregnant woman eat soft cheese or pâté?

    b Why should you always cover a cut with a plaster or dressing?

    c Why shouldn't you take ice in drinks when you are overseas on holiday?

    d After eating a meat pie, a person develops food poisoning. What bacteria might have caused the food poisoning?

    e Four hours after eating a takeaway meal containing rice, a person becomes ill. What bacteria might be the cause of this?

    f Why should you always store pre-packed salad in a refrigerator?

6 Visit the Fly on the Wall website. Watch the 8 minute video and answer these questions.

    a What was the first hygiene rule in the video?

    b Name three places where bacteria could have been transferred when the chef prepared the sandwich.

    c In the last section of the video, what did the chef use to dry his hands?

    d Why was this a good idea?

Links to this website and other websites relating to Intermediate 1 Hospitality can be found at: www.leckieandleckie.co.uk, clicking on the Learning Lab button and navigating to the Intermediate 1 Hospitality Course Notes page.

LECKIE&LECKIE
Learning Lab

Other Sources of Contamination

There are other ways in which food can become contaminated. These include:

- chemical
- metal
- physical
- plants
- fish.

> **Fertiliser:** *a natural or man-made substance which is spread on land to improve plant growth.*
> **Herbicide:** *a chemical that is used to destroy weeds.*
> **Insecticide:** *a chemical that is used to kill insects, especially those which eat plants.*

Chemical

Many different chemicals can find their way into foods. Although they are not always harmful, excessive or ongoing contamination can cause illness. Chemical contamination can come from air pollution, **fertilisers**, **herbicides** and **insecticides**.

Metal

The body requires tiny amounts of different metals such as copper, iron and zinc, for it to work properly and efficiently. However, excessive amounts of metals can be toxic.

Physical

Anything that falls into or on to food is regarded as physical contamination. Examples include a bolt or screw dropping into food from a piece of machinery/equipment or a gemstone from an item of jewellery falling into food.

Plants

Food poisoning can be caused by eating plants which are not safe to eat. The berries of some plants are poisonous, for example, deadly nightshade berries. Even familiar plants such as poppies and foxgloves have poisonous parts. Some popular vegetables can also cause food poisoning, such as:

- rhubarb – the green leaves and bud are poisonous
- potatoes – potatoes which have turned green are poisonous and must not be eaten
- mushrooms – some wild mushrooms are highly poisonous, and some mushrooms are very similar to toadstools which can also be poisonous. If you pick your own wild mushrooms, you must be very careful.

Fish

Certain types of fish, particularly shellfish, can be toxic and cause illness. This can happen if the shellfish has been feeding on poisonous plants or living in polluted waters. The puffer fish is a particularly poisonous fish; in Japan, a dish called Fugu is made from it. The puffer fish is so poisonous that, if prepared incorrectly, it can be lethal, so only licensed, trained chefs are permitted to prepare Fugu.

Food Preservation

Food is essential to human survival, so it is not surprising that food preservation is one of the oldest technologies used by human beings. The main aim of food preservation is to extend the usable life of the food by either:

- slowing down the activity of disease-causing bacteria
- killing the bacteria altogether.

In certain cases, a preservation technique may also destroy **enzymes**. Enzymes are special proteins that occur naturally in food, and they create a chemical reaction causing it to spoil or discolour quickly. They are easily destroyed by increasing the temperature of food to about 63°C.

A food that is **sterile** contains no bacteria. Unless sterilised and sealed, all food contains bacteria. For example, bacteria naturally living in milk will spoil the milk in two or three days if the milk is left at room temperature.

Putting the milk in the refrigerator doesn't kill the bacteria already there, but it does slow down their growth so that the milk will stay fresh and safe to drink for longer.

There are different ways to preserve food, including:

- controlling the temperature
- removing moisture
- altering pH.

Temperature Control Methods

Reducing the temperature

Chilling/Refrigeration

Chilling (or refrigeration) is probably one of the most popular forms of food preservation in use today. Refrigerators work at below 5°C – at this temperature, bacterial action and growth are greatly reduced, so that it takes food much longer to spoil (perhaps a week or two, rather than half a day). Refrigeration is used for almost all foods: meats, fruits, vegetables, beverages, etc. In general, and if used correctly, refrigeration has little effect on a food's taste or texture, which is why it is so popular.

Freezing

Along with chilling, freezing is probably one of the most popular forms of food preservation in use today. Freezing aims to stop bacterial action altogether. Frozen bacteria are completely inactive or dormant. Domestic freezers work at temperatures of below –18°C. Freezing is used on most foods: meats,

vegetables, fish, etc. Freezing has no effect on the taste or texture of most foods; and although it has little effect on, for example vegetables, it often completely changes the texture of fruits, which tend to become mushy when defrosted.

Increasing the temperature

Pasteurisation

If you boil a food you can kill all bacteria and make the food sterile, but you often change the taste and nutritional value of the food. **Pasteurising** a food (almost always a liquid) involves heating it to a high enough temperature to kill certain (but not all) bacteria and to destroy certain enzymes, but at the same time minimising the effects on taste as much as possible. Commonly pasteurised foods include milk, ice cream, fruit juices, beer and non-carbonated beverages. Milk, for example, can be pasteurised by heating to 62.8°C for half an hour or to 72.8°C for 15 seconds.

Ultra Heat Treatment/Ultra High Temperature (UHT)

UHT is the partial sterilisation of food, achieved by heating to a temperature of above 100°C (135–140°C) for a very short period of time, usually only 1–2 seconds. This temperature destroys many bacteria. Food that has been treated like this includes fruit juices, cream soups and milk. UHT milk can be stored, unopened for up to 9 months. Once opened, any UHT product needs to be stored under normal conditions.

Canning

For many years, **canning** has provided a way for people to preserve foods for extremely long periods of time. In canning, food is boiled in the can to kill all the bacteria and the can is then sealed (either before or while the food is boiling) to prevent any new bacteria from getting in. Since the food in the can is completely sterile, it does not spoil. Once the can is opened, bacteria enter and begin attacking the food, so the contents should be refrigerated after opening. We generally think of cans as being metal, but any sealable container, such as a glass jar, can serve as a can. One problem with canning, and a reason why refrigeration or freezing is preferred to canning, is that the act of boiling food in the can change its taste and texture (as well as its nutritional content).

Methods Involving Water Removal

Dehydration/Drying

Many foods are **dehydrated** or dried to preserve them. Traditionally foods such as fruits, fish and meat were dried in natural sunshine. Nowadays dehydrated products include:

- powdered milk
- dehydrated potatoes in a box
- dried fruits and vegetables
- dried meats
- powdered soups and sauces
- dried pasta
- instant rice.

Since most bacteria die or become completely inactive when dried, dried foods kept in air-tight containers can last quite a long time. Normally, drying completely alters the taste and texture of the food, but in many cases a completely new food is created that people like just as much as the original!

Methods Involving Altering pH

Salting

Using salt to preserve fish and meat is a very old method. Salt dries out the meat or fish, and as explained above, this lack of moisture creates conditions that bacteria do not like. If done well, salted meat can last for a long time, even years. Salt-cured ham, pastrami and corned beef are examples of salt-preserved meats.

Jam making

Sugar can be used in a similar way to salt to create conditions that bacteria do not like. The process of making jam or marmalade uses large quantities of sugar which prevent the growth of bacteria (but not always moulds or yeast).

Pickling

Pickling is a process that combines the preservative qualities of salt and acid (for example, vinegar) to create an acidic environment which hinders the growth of bacteria. Traditionally, pickling was used to preserve meats, fruits and vegetables when these items were not as widely available as they are now. Today, the pickling process is more commonly used to make 'pickles' such as pickled cucumbers, eggs or onions.

Chemicals

There are three classes of chemical preservatives commonly used in foods:

- **benzoates** (such as sodium benzoate)
- **nitrites** (such as sodium nitrite)
- **sulphites** (such as sulphur dioxide).

All of these chemicals either reduce the activity of bacteria or kill the bacteria altogether. If you look at the ingredient labels of different foods, you will frequently see these different types of chemicals used. Another common preservative that you will often see on food labels is ascorbic acid.

For you to do

7 Complete the crossword on food preservation on the Leckie and Leckie website. Go to: www.leckieandleckie.co.uk, click on the Learning Lab page and navigate to the Intermediate 1 Hospitality page.

LECKIE&LECKIE
Learning Lab

Food Storage

The golden rule for good food safety is to always store food:

- in the right place
- at the right temperature
- for the right time.

Food items are commonly stored in fridges, freezers, cupboards and vegetable racks.

Fridges

Perishable foods are normally stored in the fridge. There are rules that should be followed to make sure that food stored in the fridge will continue to be safe to eat.

Rules for storing food in the fridge

1 Store cooked and raw foods separately in the fridge. This prevents cross-contamination.

2 Keep raw foods at the lower part of the fridge. This prevents fluids dropping from raw to cooked foods in the fridge.

3 Cover all foods. This prevents food from drying out, stops odours transferring from one food to another, and prevents direct contact between foods.

4 Eggs should be kept in the fridge in their box.

5 Almost all foods (except dried foods) should be stored in the fridge once opened. Transfer such foods on to a clean dish, cover them and ideally label them to help you know how long the food has been opened. Such foods should be used within 2 days, or according to the instructions on the label.

6 Never overfill the fridge. Cool air needs to circulate round stored foods in order to ensure that they remain below 5°C.

7 Never place warm foods in the fridge. This increases the internal temperature of the fridge and so makes it work less efficiently. Bacteria may be able to multiply more quickly.

8 Always store foods in the correct part of the fridge.

For you to do

8 You have been asked to store the following items in the fridge:

cheese, dairy products   salad

uncooked red meats and sausages   cooked meat

uncooked poultry   pies, pâté, etc.

List where you should place them, starting with the top shelf. If you need help, visit the Foster UK website.

9 Use the Foster UK website to find out how long you should store each of the following foods in a fridge:

a uncooked steak   **b** uncooked minced meat

c uncooked sausages   **d** cooked chicken

e cooked mince pies   **f** pâté.

For links to this site and other websites relating to Intermediate 1 Hospitality, go to: www.leckieandleckie.co.uk, click on the Learning Lab page and navigate to the Intermediate 1 Hospitality page.

Freezers

Most foods can be frozen safely (exceptions include canned food or eggs in shells). However, some foods – such as cream and fruit/vegetables with a high water content such as lettuce and strawberries – don't freeze and defrost well, so are best kept fresh.

With freezing, you can store foods for a very long time. However, eventually the quality of the food will start to deteriorate. There are rules that should be followed to make sure that food stored in the freezer will continue to be safe to eat.

Rules for storing food in the freezer

1 If foods are fresh and in the best condition at the time of freezing, they will taste better than foods frozen near the end of their useful life.

2 Make sure that food being frozen is wrapped appropriately. This helps to maintain the quality of the frozen food as well as preventing **freezer burn** (caused by air penetrating poor packaging and reaching the surface of the food). Freezer burn does not make food unsafe for use, but it does affect the look and texture as it causes dry, grey-brown patches.

3 Try to freeze food as quickly as possible as this maintains its quality. Rapid freezing forms small ice crystals throughout the food item, whereas slow freezing creates larger ice crystals which damage the cell structure of the food during thawing. This can result in an unappealing texture, such as soggy strawberries.

4   All food stored in the freezer should be labelled with the date of packing so that you can identify how long food has been frozen.

5   Never refreeze food which has been defrosted. During defrosting, bacteria will have had time to multiply, so if you refreeze the food, you will freeze an increased number of bacteria.

For you to do

10   You have been asked to store the following foods in a freezer:

a	ice cream	**b**	chicken pieces
c	cooked, leftover meat	**d**	apples
e	pineapple	**f**	cauliflower
g	doughnuts	**h**	fruit pie
i	fresh milk	**j**	hard-boiled eggs

You have also been asked to complete a log-book at the same time.

Visit the Clemson website to find the recommended maximum storage time for each item, and work out the latest date each item can safely be stored until.

For links to this site and other websites relating to Intermediate 1 Hospitality, go to: www.leckieandleckie.co.uk, click on the Learning Lab page and navigate to the Intermediate 1 Hospitality page.

Cupboards

Store cupboards are an ideal place for storing unopened cans, packets and some jars and bottles. Again, there are rules to ensure that food stored in cupboards remains at best quality.

Rules for storing food in the freezer

1   Cupboards should be dry, particularly if dried foods are to be stored. Opened packets or dried foods should be securely sealed before storage to prevent moisture getting into the product and so allowing bacteria to multiply.

2   Store cans in a clean, dry cupboard. Dented, bashed or rusted cans should always be thrown away.

3   Any unused contents from cans should be transferred into a clean container, covered and then stored in a refrigerator.

4   Keep cupboards clean and remove all spills and crumbs immediately so they don't attract insects and breed bacteria.

Vegetable rack

Different types of fruits and vegetables require different types of storage. Generally, root vegetables such as potatoes, turnips and carrots benefit from being stored in a cool dark place. In most cases fruits and vegetables should be removed from any plastic packaging in which they were bought.

Additional help with storage times

No food lasts forever, no matter well it is stored. Most pre-packed foods carry either a **Use by date** or a **Best before date**. Check food labels carefully, and look out for advice on how long food can be kept once the packaging has been opened.

USE BY
8 OCTOBER

BEST BEFORE
13 JULY 2008

- Use by dates: these are used for highly perishable foods – those that 'go off' quite quickly. It can be dangerous to eat foods past their use by date and it is against the law for a retailer to sell food that is past its use by date.

- Best before dates: these are used for foods with a longer life. They indicate how long the food will be at its best quality. You can still eat food which has gone beyond its best before date but the flavour, texture, colour and/or smell will not be as good as when the product was first packed.

Hints and Tips

Remember the golden rule: Use up older items first (first in, first out).

If in doubt, throw it out!

The Law and Food Safety

Important laws are in place to protect consumers when they buy food, whether from the supermarket, shops, hotels or restaurants. The law covers all places that sell food – even the burger van and vending machines.

There are two main pieces of food safety legislation:

- The Food Safety Act 1990
- The Food Hygiene (Scotland) Regulations 2006.

The Food Safety Act 1990

The Food Safety Act is a wide-ranging law which affects everyone involved in the production, processing, storage, distribution or sale of food. It applies to all food premises.

Main requirements

- Food must be of the nature, substance or quality described – for example, food described as cod must be cod and not hake, and food should not be sold if it contains a foreign object.
- Food must not be falsely or misleadingly described – for example, it must not make false claims about a food product's health benefits.
- Food must not cause injury to health – for example, food must not have something added to it or removed from it which could cause harm to anyone who consumes it.
- Food must not be unfit – for example, food must not have decomposed and become putrid or 'off'.
- Food must not be so contaminated that it would be unreasonable to expect it to be eaten – for example, food which contains high quantities of chemicals.

Officers' powers

The Act also provides Environmental Health Officers with powers of enforcement, which include:

- seizing foods which are regarded as unfit, etc.
- issuing Improvement Notices on owners of businesses that fail to meet the hygiene standards laid down in the regulations
- issuing Prohibition Orders to prohibit the use of an unsafe process/treatment
- issuing Emergency Prohibition Notices to close any premises which is causing a real risk to health.

Defence

The Act provides a defence for owners of food businesses to prove that they took all reasonable precautions and exercised all possible steps to avoid the cause of the offence, by themselves or a person under their control.

The Food Hygiene (Scotland) Regulations 2006

The Food Hygiene (Scotland) Regulations are based on European Union food safety laws which specify certain safety standards for the processing and sale of food. It is an offence for anyone to process or sell food which is harmful to health. The regulations also place an obligation on businesses to ensure that their activities are carried out in a hygienic way and that good structural standards are in place, including training of food handlers. Running a food business means that you have a particular responsibility to protect the health of your customers.

From 1 January 2006, food businesses must have established written procedures based on the principles of hazard analysis critical control point (HACCP). This means that a food producer has to identify possible food safety risks, put in place measures to prevent these risks from taking place, and then review and evaluate all potential risks on a regular basis.

Temperature Control

If food temperature is not regulated carefully, bacteria can multiply rapidly, seriously affecting food safety. For this reason, the law describes requirements for cooking and holding food at specific temperatures.

The law specifies that food must:

- be kept refrigerated or
- be kept in a cool ventilated place or
- be kept at a temperature above 63°C or
- if being reheated, be kept at a temperature above 82°C.

For you to do

11 Design a poster with the following title:

Keep Hot Food Hot – Keep Cold Food Cold

The Food Premises

Food law also make specific rules and regulations about the design of all food premises, whether an actual building or a mobile fast food van.

Cleaning and disinfection

- The layout and design should allow for easy cleaning and disinfection – where dirt is likely to build up, it should be easy to clean.
- Areas which are likely to be hot or steamy need special attention to prevent the build-up of mould and condensation.
- Care must be taken to prevent any possible cross-contamination by pests, visitors and workers.
- Surfaces, including equipment, which will come into contact with both raw and cooked foods should be well cleaned before and after use.
- Floors, walls and other surfaces (ceilings, doors and windows) must be kept in a good condition and must be easy to clean and disinfect.
- Windows which can be opened must be fitted with insect-proof screens; these should be easy to remove for cleaning.

Wash hand basins

- The number of hand washing basins should be suitable for the number of employees.
- Wash hand basins should be used for hand washing only, and should have both running hot and cold water, soap and paper towels for hand drying.
- Hand basins should be located close to the toilet facilities.

Toilets

- There should be one toilet for every five employees.
- All toilet facilities must be ventilated and should not lead directly into a food preparation area.

Ventilation and lighting

- Ventilation must be provided to make sure that there is no build-up of heat that can lead to bacterial growth.
- Lighting must allow for good food handling and food safety.

Changing facilities

- Changing facilities should be provided, where necessary, to allow food handlers to change from outdoor clothing into protective clothing.

Water supply

- There should be an adequate supply of drinkable (potable) water.

Food waste

■ Food waste should not be allowed to build up in food preparation areas, and should be disposed of regularly.

■ Food waste containers should have a closable lid and be easy to clean and disinfect.

Pests

Because pests carry dirt, disease and bacteria, legislation requires that owners of food businesses take all reasonable action to prevent pests entering food premises. The most common pests that cause **infestation** problems in food premises include: rodents (mice and rats), insects (flies, wasps, bluebottles, cockroaches and ants) and birds (often pigeons).

Infestation: *the state of being overrun by pests.*

For you to do

12 Visit the school dining centre and make notes about each of these areas:

■ the type of work surfaces in the food preparation area

■ the type of floor covering in the kitchen food preparation area

■ the temperature of the chiller cabinets or refrigerator (you may need permission to do this)

■ the type of ventilation in the kitchen area.

Cleaning schedules

Clean food premises, work surfaces and equipment are essential to maintain good food safety and hygiene.

In all food premises, food safety inspectors will visit regularly to check that premises are clean and hygienic. The inspectors will ask to see a record of cleaning schedules. These are the procedures that the food business uses to clean all equipment and dishes. A cleaning schedule will usually record:

■ the item/area to be cleaned

■ how often the item/area has to be cleaned

■ what method of cleaning has to be used

■ the date the last clean was undertaken

■ the signature of the person who is responsible for the cleaning.

CHAPTER 1
KITCHEN ORGANISATION

2 a The task is to make a 1-portion fruit cooler.
  b The component parts are: 1 orange, 5 ml lemon juice, 250 ml water, 5 ml caster sugar, 2 ice cubes.
  c There are 7 processes: collect, wash, cut, place, liquidise, drain, serve.

3

Times	Activities	Notes
2.00 – 2.05	Wash hands. Collect all ingredients for the fruit cooler.	
2.05 – 2.10	Place glasses in freezer to chill. Prepare orange and place into liquidiser with other ingredients.	
2.10 – 2.15	Liquidise and drain liquid.	
2.15 – 2.20	Clean and tidy work area. Serve drink into chilled glasses.	

4

FOOD REQUISITION SHEET

Name: .... Class: ....

Teacher: .... Date required:.....................

Item(s) to be made: ....

Meat and Fish Chicken thighs	Quantity 8	Fruit and Vegetables Celery Lettuce Seedless grapes Melon	Quantity 2 sticks 1/2 225g 1 small
Dairy Products Butter	Quantity 30g	Tins/Bottles/Dried Tarragon vinegar Olive oil	Quantity 30ml 50ml
Other foods Rosemary Chicken stock	Quantity Sprigs 150ml	Equipment and Resources Microwave oven Pepper mill grinder	

5

RECIPE COSTING SHEET

Dish: ....

Portions required:............ 2 .... Recipe portions:............ 4 ....

Ingredients	Recipe measures		Actual measures		Costing	
	Units	Millilitres/Grams	Units	Millilitres/Grams	Unit/Litre/kg price	Total cost
Margarine	100	g	50	g	50p/500g	£0.05
Self-raising flour	100	g	50	g	50p/1500g	£0.02
Caster sugar	100	g	50	g	75p/1000g	£0.04
Eggs	2		1		100p for 10	£0.10
					Cost	£0.21
					Cost per portion	£0.11

CHAPTER 2
FOOD PREPARATION

1 a scales
  c scales
  e scales
  b jug/measuring cup
  d measuring spoon
  f measuring spoon

2 a
½ of 50g = 25g

  b
½ of 25g = 12.5g

5 Types of nozzles include (the list isn't exhaustive): *plain* – writing and lines; *rope* – rope effect; *star* – star effect; *leaf* – leaves; *basket weave* – basket effect; *petal* – for flowers/petals; *calligraphy* – for writing; *grass/hair* – grass/hair effect.

6 Note: these answers are not exhaustive.
  a Vegetable peeler, vegetable knife, citrus peeler
  b Grater, mouli grater, flat grater, food processor
  c Cook's knife, vegetable knife
  d Cook's knife, grater, food processor
  e Biscuit/dough cutter, rolling pin, knife, flan rings, cake tins, piping bag
  f Rolling pin
  g Rotary whisk, flat whisk, hand-held electric whisk, balloon whisk, ball whisk
  h Tablespoon, wooden spoon, fork, round-bladed knife
  i Piping bag, piping tube
  j Mixing bowl and wooden spoon, hand-held electric whisk, food processor

7 a A mandolin is used to slice food thinly.
  b A French fry cutter is used to cut root vegetables into chip shapes.
  c A sausage stuffer is used to stuff sausages into sausage skins.

8 a Knead
  c Whisk
  b Glaze
  d Cream

9 b 10 b 11 b 12 c

13 a *Brunoise:* small cubes, usually about 2mm along each side.
  b *Mise en place:* preparation prior to cooking or serving.
  c *Flambé:* to set on fire using a spirit such as brandy during the cooking process.
  d *Chiffonade:* finely cut strips of food, for example, lettuce.

14 There are no correct answers but the following would be appropriate:
  a, b, c Very frequently and certainly after each use.
  d Minimum once a day
  e When required and certainly if preventing good lighting. Minimum once every 2 weeks.
  f At the end of each day as a minimum.

CHAPTER 3
COOKERY PROCESSES

1   a   *Conduction* – through the metal tin and through the food; *convection* – movement of hot and cold air inside the oven.

    b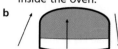

2   a   4–6 mins   b   8–10 mins   c   12–16 mins   d   12 mins
    e   2–3 mins   f   12–15 mins   g   2–3 mins   h   20–25 mins

3   Chill lobster for 4–5 hours before cooking. Place it (live) into a pan of boiling water. Bring water back to the boil and boil for 15 minutes. (Note: live lobsters are bought with their claws tied with elastic bands. Do not remove these.) Some people regard this as a cruel method of cooking. It is believed that chilling numbs the lobster and so there should be no pain. (However, this argument is not accepted by everyone.) Remember that a chef has to be able to cook foods that customers actually want and will pay for. Sometimes this might go against your personal thoughts and beliefs.

5   a   A   b   D   c   D   d   A   e   NR   f   NR

6   These answers are illustrative only – there are many more answers that could be accepted:
    A – asparagus; B – bream (a fish); C – chicken fillet;
    D – damsons (a type of fruit); E – eggs.

8   a   Splitting large quantities of foods into batches for cooking.
    b   Steam cabinets used to help yeast dough products to rise.
    c   Term used to measure the quality of the surface appearance of a finished product.
    d   The process of applying a coating to a cake.
    e   A fat used in pastry making, for example.
    f   Time for a dough mix or pastry to settle or rest before cooking, to prevent shrinkage during cooking in the oven.

9   These answers are illustrative only – there are many more answers that could be accepted: A – apples, apricots;
    F – figs; G – gooseberries, greengages; N – nectarines;
    P – peaches, pears, pineapples.

10 a   Fat drips from the food when being grilled.
    b   5 cm
    c   6–8 minutes
    d   The thickness of the meat and the degree of cooking required.
    e   Creamy garlic and herb; pesto; creamy chilli; stilton and watercress.

11 *Breadcrumbs:* used to coat the fish prior to cooking, providing an outer covering.
    Egg: used to bind the breadcrumbs to the fish.
    Flour: used to dry coat the food to enable the egg to stick to the fish.
    Salt and pepper: used to season the food.

12 a   below 5°C   b   above 63°C
    c   above 82°C   d   below 5°C
    e   above 63°C   f   below 5°C
    g   over 82°C

CHAPTER 4
FOOD SAFETY

3   a   Between 5 and 63°C
    b   Above 63°C
    c   Below 5°C
    d   Below 0°C

4   a, b, e, g

5   a   They may contain listeria which can damage an unborn baby.
    b   It may contain *Staphylococcus* bacteria which would contaminate food.
    c   The ice cubes may be a potential source of dysentery/typhoid/*listeria*/*campylobacter*/ *E.coli 0157*/*salmonella*.
    d   *Clostridium perfringens*/*staphylococcus aureus*/*salmonella*/*E.coli*/*campylobacter*/listeria.
    e   *Bacillus cereus*.
    f   It may contain *listeria*; keeping the food cool will prevent multiplication.

6   a   Wash your hands properly.
    b   Apron, jug, plates, dish towel, bread, filling, knife, chopping board.
    c   Paper towel.
    d   Good because the towel is thrown away and so any possible cross-contamination is prevented.

8   The foods should be stored in this order, starting with the top shelf: cheese, dairy products; cooked meat; salad; pies, pâté, etc.; uncooked red meats and sausages; uncooked poultry

9   a   2 day   b   1 day   c   3 days
    d   2 days   e   1 day   f   2 days

10 Add the following maximum storage time to today's date:
    a   2 months   b   9–12 months
    c   2–3 months   d   8–12 months
    e   4–6 months   f   8–12 months
    g   3 months   h   1 year
    I   not recommended   j   not recommended

Glossary

bake blind bake without a filling (p. 44)

baking method of cooking in which prepared food is cooked in a pre-heated oven (p. 60)

baste spoon fat or liquid over food to keep it moist (p. 44)

beat add a small amount of air to a mixture using a spoon or fork (p. 44)

blanch dip food ingredients into boiling water for a short time before cooling quickly (p. 44)

blend combine two or more ingredients together, normally a dry and a liquid ingredient, to form a smooth paste (p. 44)

boil method of cooking in which prepared food is cooked in a liquid (p. 52)

Bratt pan industrial cooking appliance used to produce large quantities of cooked food (p. 53)

chef de partie chef in charge of a section of work in the kitchen (pp. 6–7)

coat cover food to protect it when cooking (p. 44)

commis chef assistant cook to a chef de partie (pp. 6–7)

components ingredients of a recipe (p. 10)

conduction process of transferring heat through a hot solid surface directly on to a cold solid surface (pp. 48–9)

confectionery sweets or chocolate (p. 56)

contact grill grill used for grilling over and under food at the same time (p. 62)

contamination (cross-contamination) the act of contaminating food (pp. 78–9)

convection the process of transferring heat either through liquid or through air (p. 49)

cooking medium liquid that is used to assist in the transfer of heat, e.g. water, oil (p. 50)

cook's knife (chef's knife / French knife) all-purpose kitchen knife used for most types of chopping, dicing and slicing (p. 29)

cooling tray tray used for cooling hot cooked foods on all sides after being baked (p. 26)

cream mix ingredients together, especially fat and sugar (p. 42, 44)

dash a small amount of an ingredient (p. 22)

decorate add attractive ingredients to a sweet dish before serving (p. 44)

dry cooking method cooking that does not require the use of a liquid (p. 51)

electric food processor kitchen tool used for many processes (p. 26)

fish slice kitchen tool used to turn over or remove cooked items from pans (p. 26)

flake divide into small bits (p. 44)

flash heat to heat something quickly (p. 63)

flour dredger metal container with a cover/lid that has small holes punched in it (p. 27)

fold gently mix ingredients together with a metal spoon to prevent air loss (p. 44)

food hygiene practices that prevent contamination of food (pp. 70–1)

food preservation extending the usable life of food (pp. 80–3)

Food Safety Act law governing all aspects of commercial food handling (p. 88)

food storage the storing of food in a safe and appropriate place (pp. 84–7)

fricassée dish made of pieces of meat cooked and served in a white sauce (p. 55)

garnish decorate a savoury dish (p. 44)

glaze give a shine, usually to baked or roasted foods (p. 44)

grate rub solid food items against a grating instrument to produce smaller pieces (p. 40)

grater kitchen tool that grates and shreds food finely (pp. 27–8)

griddle cook items on a lightly oiled metal plate (p. 65)

grill quick method of cooking in which food is cooked with very intense and direct heat (pp. 62–3)

handy measures quick way to measure ingredients approximately (p. 23)

head chef the chef in charge of, and with ultimate responsibility for, the kitchen (pp. 6–7)

heaped tablespoon handy ingredient measure that means as much ingredient as possible on the spoon without it falling off (p. 23)

hotpot dish of meats, vegetables and potatoes cooked slowly in a covered dish (p. 60)

imperial measurements old system of measurement using ounces and pounds (p. 20)

industrial equipment equipment found in professional kitchens that can process large quantities of food and is strong enough to withstand heavy and frequent use (p. 43)

julienne peeler fruit and vegetable peeler used to make julienne strips (p. 39)

julienne strips thin strips of fruit and vegetables used as garnishes (p. 39)

knead gently handle a pastry or dough mixture before rolling out or shaping (p. 44)

level tablespoon handy ingredient measure that indicates that the ingredient is level with the top edge of the spoon (p. 23)

measuring cups cups of various sizes used to measure single amounts of dry, solid or liquid ingredients (p. 21)

measuring jug container with a spout, a handle and a graduated scale on the side used to measure liquid quantities (p. 21)

measuring spoons set of spoons used to measure small quantities of dry and liquid ingredients (pp. 20–1)

metric measurements system of measuring ingredients using grams (g), kilograms (kg), millilitres (ml) and litres (l) (p. 20)

micro-organisms organisms like bacteria, moulds, yeasts and viruses, some of which can cause illness if present in foods (pp. 72–3)

mix combine ingredients so that they are all distributed evenly within the mixture (p. 42)

orange peeler small, narrow utensil designed to remove peels from citrus fruits (p. 38)

palette knife blunt-style knife used for shaping and turning foods and finishing surfaces (p. 30)

pare remove the skin or rind (p. 44)

partie system system for organising a professional kitchen into different sections which perform specific tasks (pp. 6–7)

pastry brush brush used to apply glazing to items before or after baking (p. 30)

pastry cutter hand-held tool used to cut evenly shaped pieces from dough (p. 30)

pastry wheel kitchen utensil used for cutting pastry dough as it is prepared for baking (p. 31)

peel the removal of the outer skin or rind of a fruit or vegetable (p. 38)

perishable spoils quickly (p. 75)

pinch measurement indicating the amount of dry ingredient you can hold between your forefinger and thumb (p. 22)

pipe squeeze a piping bag to force soft mixtures through the tip of the bag to decorate or create special shapes (p. 41)

piping bag (pastry bag / icing bag) cone-shaped bag that can be filled with a soft mixture (p. 31)

pith white layer of skin located directly underneath the zest of a citrus fruit (p. 38)

plain tube (nozzle) small or large tool attached to small end of piping bag through which mixture is forced (p. 34)

poach method of cooking in which prepared food is cooked in a liquid at a temperature below boiling point (pp. 46–7)

processes steps that have to be undertaken to complete a task such as a recipe (p. 10)

pulp soft, wet mass of cooked fruit (p. 55)

purée make a smooth thick paste (p. 44)

radiation the direct transfer of heat on to the surface of food (pp. 49–50)

ratatouille savoury dish made by cooking vegetables in a liquid over a slow heat (p. 55)

reduce thicken a sauce by boiling it (p. 65)

requisition(ing) ordering (pp. 14–15)

roll out make a dough thinner and smoother ready for shaping using a rolling pin (p. 40)

rolling pin long, cylindrical kitchen utensil used to roll out various types of dough (p. 32)

rotary grater (mouli grater) hand-held utensil that consists of a turning mechanism with a grating surface (p. 28)

rounded tablespoon handy ingredient measure that means there is as much of the ingredient you are measuring above the top edge of the spoon as there is in the bowl of the spoon (p. 23)

salamander grill grill used for overhead grilling of meat (p. 62)

sauté pan pan with vertical sides used for shallow frying of meat and potatoes (p. 64)

sauter (sauté) shallow fry and use a tossing action when turning the food (p. 64)

sauteuse pan pan with sloping sides used for reducing sauces (p. 64)

scales (balance, spring, digital) kitchen device used to measure the weight of ingredients and other foods (p. 22)

season add salt and pepper (p. 44)

shallow fry fast method of cooking where prepared food is cooked in a pre-heated pan with a small amount of fat or oil (pp. 64–5)

shape take food ingredients and form them into an appropriate shape (pp. 40–1)

sieve kitchen utensil used to strain liquid or to sift dry ingredients (p. 32)

sous chef assistant to the head chef (pp. 6–7)

star tube tube that gives textured finish to ingredients piped through a piping bag (p. 34)

steam method of cooking where prepared food is cooked in steam (pp. 58–9)

stew method of cooking in which prepared food is cooked in, and served with, a small amount of cooking liquid (p. 55)

stir fry cook fish, meats or vegetables quickly in oil (p. 65)

strain remove solid food from a liquid (p. 44)

sweat fry items slowly in a little fat, using a lid and without allowing the food to colour (p. 65)

tablespoon handy ingredient measure; also, kitchen utensil used for mixing, stirring or folding ingredients together, (p. 23, 33)

task a piece of work to be undertaken or completed (p. 10)

tube (nozzle) tool placed into the small end of a piping bag through which mixture is forced (p. 34)

veal meat from a calf (p. 55)

vegetable knife (paring knife) small knife used to trim and shape vegetables (p. 29)

vegetable peeler kitchen tool used to remove very thin layers of skin or flesh from vegetables and firm fruits (p. 35)

wet cooking method cooking that requires the use of a liquid (p. 51)

whip beat briskly (p. 44)

whisk blend ingredients together or to incorporate air into ingredients (p. 42)

whisks – ball, balloon, electric, flat, rotary (pp. 36–7)

wok Chinese pan used for fast frying food (p. 64)

zest outer skin of a citrus fruit (p. 38)

zesting removal of a very fine amount of skin from a citrus fruit by grating finely (p. 28)

Conversion Charts

Use the conversion charts here to help you convert unfamiliar measurements you may find in recipes. There are more charts on the Leckie and Leckie website.

You should never mix measurements when using recipes. Always use either the metric or imperial quantities for ingredients.

When ordering foods or writing out your recipes for your Practical Cookery course, you must use **metric** measurements. If you are not sure how to convert from one measure to the other, use the charts here or go to the Convert-Me website. A link to this site is given on the Leckie and Leckie website.

For charts and website links, go to: **www.leckieandleckie.co.uk**, click on the Learning Lab button and navigate to the Intermediate 1 Hospitality Course Notes page.

Oven temperatures

Gas mark	$^1/_4$	$^1/_2$	1	2	3	4	5	6	7	8	9
°Fahrenheit	225	250	275	300	325	350	375	400	425	450	475
°Celsius	110	130	140	150	170	180	190	200	220	230	240
Description	Very cool / very slow		cool		very moderate	moderate		moderately hot		hot	very hot

Conversion guides

Weights

Metric to imperial

1 gram (g) = 1000 mg = 0.0353 ounces
1 kilogram (kg) = 1000 g = 2.2046 pounds

Imperial to metric

1 ounce (oz) = 28.35 g
1 pound (lb) = 16 ounces = 0.4536 kg
1 stone (st) = 14 lb = 6.3503 kg

Liquids

Metric to imperial

15 ml = $^1/_2$ fl. oz
30 ml = 1 fl. oz
500 ml = 18 fl. oz
1 litre = 1.76 pt

Imperial to metric

$^1/_2$ fl. oz = 15 ml
1 fl. oz = 30 ml
5 fl. oz = $^1/_4$ pint (pt) = 150 ml
10 fl. oz = $^1/_2$ pt = 300 ml
20 fl. oz = 1pt = 600 ml

Exact conversions for liquids

1 litre = 35.21 fl. oz = 1.76 pt
5 millilitres = 0.176 fl. oz

1 pint = 568 ml
1 fl. oz = 28.4 ml